THE SILENT CITIES
Civilizations
Lost and Found

Mildred
Boyd

THE
SILENT
CITIES

*Civilizations
Lost
and
Found*

CRITERION BOOKS
NEW YORK

By the same author
BLACK FLAGS AND PIECES OF EIGHT
HISTORY IN HARNESS: The Story of Horses

To my daughters,
Kathy, Tina and Judy
for whom this book
was written

Acknowledgments

The photographs in this book are reproduced through the courtesy of:

Wide World Photos, Inc. —
  1. Temples of a Lost Civilization   16
  2. Ancient City Unearthed   27
  3. Queen Nefertiti   47
  4. Newlyweds — Sixth century B.C.   102

Free Lance Photographers Guild —
  1. Zimbabwe Ruins   123

All others from the N.Y. Public Library.

Contents

Illustrations

1 The Silent Cities Speak

The earth, according to the latest estimates, is between four and five billion years old. Man, as a separate and distinct species, is no more than one and a half million years old. He has been living in communities and recording his history for less than six thousand years. Yet in that comparatively short time, countless civilizations have risen, flourished briefly, and vanished from sight. Their territories have been overrun, their cities deserted, their peoples killed or scattered, and their languages forgotten.

All over the world we have found them — the silent cities, the royal palaces hidden beneath shifting desert sands, the mighty temples swallowed up in steaming jungles, the great monuments buried beneath the garbage heaps of later cities.

How can one lose a city? There are many ways.

Herculaneum and Pompeii lay for centuries beneath the mud and ash of a volcanic eruption. Though the manner of their dying was dramatic enough to be long remembered, the location of the cities themselves was soon forgotten.

Mighty Knossos died on a spring day when a strong

13

wind blew from the southwest. Some scientists believe that
Crete was shattered by earthquakes. Perhaps, as so often
happened, it was human invaders who destroyed the Cretan
civilization. Geologists have advanced the theory that
volcanic ash, thrown up by an eruption on a small island
north of Crete, fell on Knossos, poisoning the atmosphere.
Whatever it was, Knossos lay as she had fallen, while countless generations lived and died and planted their olive
groves on her grave.

Angkor Thom was abandoned to the encroaching jungles
of Cambodia; Tikal and Chichen Itza to those of Guatemala
and Yucatan. In the long centuries before accident revealed
their presence, their silence was disturbed only by the cries
of wild animals.

Ur of the Chaldees, Babylon, Ninevah, Troy — the list is a
long one — all were destroyed by the enemies that besieged
their walls, and their people were killed or driven into
slavery.

Even the monumental tombs and temples of Egypt, far
too large to be hidden completely from view, were washed
by the sands of the desert until no one remembered pre-
cisely why they were built, much less when.

Rome built her cities, her aqueducts, her wonderful roads
to the limits of her far-flung domains. But long before the
Eastern Empire fell to the Moslem hordes, most of them
were forgotten ruins.

Men have built cities in the depths of tropical jungles, on
inaccessible mountain peaks, in deep gorges, in the empty
vastness of the desert and in the middle of lakes. Many will
probably never be known, for they were built of materials

which decayed in time and left no trace. Only those constructed of stone or brick, or preserved by favorable
climates, have survived. Even so, there are hundreds of
known ruins scattered around the globe.

Until every one of them has been subjected to the rigid
scrutiny of qualified men and women, we can make no more
than tentative guesses about that most fascinating of all
subjects — the origins of human civilization. All too many of
these sites have never received more than a cursory examination by the experts.

Some are well-known and have been thoroughly investigated by teams of scientists. A handful are familiar to the
general public, usually because of the mystery or drama of
their discoveries or the light they shed on time-honored
legends.

These are the ones whose names ring like a clarion call
across the centuries.

Babylon! Who has not heard of that glittering and sinful
city? Our Bible is filled with stories of her power and pride,
her wealth and her wickedness. Though she lay long in
ruins, the great city was never really lost. The heap of
sun-dried rubble, 25 miles south of Baghdad, was still
called Babil by the natives when Claudius Rich discovered
inscribed bricks there in 1811.

Still, until 1899, when Dr. Robert Koldewey dug into the
mound and revealed the mighty walls, broad avenues, and
towering temples of brick and glazed tile, Babylon was
considered a lost city.

Now, after more than half a century of excavation and
painstaking restoration, the great Ishtar gate stands re-

Angkor Thom, a busy city for six hundred years, now lies abandoned in the jungles of Cambodia.

vealed in all its ancient glory. The houses and palaces and temples are clearly outlined. And we know a great deal about how the people lived in those far-off days before the Children of Israel were carried into slavery. We know where the fabulous hanging gardens stood. We have even discovered the magnificent many-tiered ziggurat, the original Tower of Babel!

Knossos! The beautiful city of the Sea Kings of Crete stands today as a monument to one man above all others. Sir Arthur Evans devoted his life to the excavation and his fortune to the preservation of the sprawling complex of buildings he called the Palace of Minos. Through his efforts modern man can know intimately a people whose civilization died in the wind-fanned flames of that spring day in 1400 B.C.

We know the lovely ladies of the court with their elaborate hair styles and their flounced skirts. We can see the daring feats of the bull leapers as they somersault over the wicked horns of the charging beasts. We can stand in solemn awe before the subterranean altar of the mother-goddess whose symbol of the double axe dominates the palace decor. And we feel again the long-vanished power of these sophisticated islanders who were, in many ways, surprisingly modern.

Troy! The celebrated city of Homer's *Iliad* was long believed to be no more than a figment of the poet's imagination. Not until Heinrich Schliemann, who believed passionately that every word that Homer wrote was true, would anyone bother to make a real search for the "mythical" city.

In many ways Schliemann's life story is as fascinating as the legends of the Trojan war. His rise from humble beginnings, to become a millionaire several times over and achieve his boyhood dream of finding Priam's fabled city, makes reading as exciting as anything Homer recorded. As a climax to his true-life adventure, he even discovered a fabulous treasure in golden ornaments!

Unfortunately, in the great layer cake mound of Hissarlik, Schliemann's eager thumb pulled out the wrong plum. The occupation stratum he identified as the city of Homer actually belonged to a people who had vanished centuries before the Greek armies sailed in pursuit of the fair Helen and her kidnapper.

There are many cities piled one above the other in the mound of Hissarlik. Schliemann had dug right through the city of Priam at level VIIa and declared Troy II, second from the bottom, to be the real Troy. No matter; Troy *was* found, and a new chapter was added to our history.

Pompeii! Buried alive in the ash from a cataclysmic eruption of Vesuvius in A.D. 79, she is perhaps the most fascinating of all lost cities. Ordinarily only palaces and temples and state buildings have survived the ravages of time. But Pompeii has preserved for us the tiniest details of the life of an Italian city in the first century after Christ.

The houses and their furnishings, the wine shops, the bakeries with their round, flat loaves, the tools of the craftsmen, even the political slogans painted on the walls emerge intact from the grip of cemented ash. It is almost as if the city had lain under an enchantment for nearly two thousand years.

Angkor! When naturalist Henri Mouhot parted the tangled vines which formed a living wall and gazed for the first time on the towers and terraces of that fantastic city, he forgot all about the rare butterflies which had brought him to the jungles of Cambodia.

He was the first white man to look upon the vast plazas surrounded by miles of carved walls and deep moats. He saw lotus pools reflecting the thousands of pillars and columns festooned with intricate carving and intertwined with the living green of the vines which cascaded from every facade. And, rising from the center, he saw the great temple with its tiers of stone lace surmounted by soaring spires from which four great faces of Buddha gazed serenely over the jungle in all directions.

Perhaps he was more than a little inclined to believe it when the natives told him the silent city had been built by the gods! We know better, thanks to the archaeologists who have excavated there for nearly a century. Actually, Angkor was built by a people called the Khmers.

When it was discovered in 1841, it had already been abandoned for over four hundred years. Early in the ninth century A.D., a powerful Khmer ruler succeeded in uniting the quarreling Cambodians under his authority, but the city of Angkor Thom was not founded until A.D. 899. Successive kings added to its glories, culminating in the magnificent temple of Angkor Wat, largest of all the city's buildings. Angkor was sacked by the invading Chams soon after, but was rebuilt on an even grander scale.

But the wars raged on, and Angkor was abandoned forever in 1432.

Chichen Itza! The sacred city of the Maya, with its terrible well of sacrifice, has fascinated archaeologists and laymen alike ever since it was discovered by Edward Herbert Thompson in 1885.

Thompson's adventures in the wilds of Yucatan surpass even Schliemann's for pure excitement. His descent into the depths of the sacred *cenote* in a diving suit was as daring and dangerous a feat as archaeology has ever known.

Legend stated that human sacrifice was made regularly to the Maya rain god who lived in the murky waters of the great natural well. The victims were thrown from the edge of a ceremonial platform and fell 65 feet to the fearsome pool below. Thompson proved the truth of the legend by recovering human skeletons, as well as objects of gold, silver, and jade. The inky-black waters at the bottom of the well of sacrifice yielded a real treasure, but its scientific value far exceeded its monetary worth.

Thompson went on to discover a secret burial chamber beneath one of the pyramids, the first ever discovered in Central America.

His spectacular finds aroused such interest in pre-Columbian art and culture that today Chichen Itza is one of the best known of the "lost cities," and Mayan history is emerging bit by bit from the darkness into which it was plunged by the fanaticism of the Spanish priests four centuries ago.

We know now that the ruined cities of Guatemala and Yucatan were never real cities. They appear to have been no more than ceremonial centers, dedicated to the gods and occupied only by the men who served those gods, the priests. They were also the seats of the amazing Mayan learning.

Their strange religious beliefs prompted an intense interest in the passage of time and inspired the development of a fantastically accurate calendar. They also necessitated a broad knowledge of astronomy, which in turn demanded a writing system to record their observations. Unfortunately, all but three Mayan books were destroyed by the Spaniards, and we can read little but dates from their numerous carved inscriptions.

Most of the Mayan sites were abandoned long before Columbus set sail. We do not know why. But the descendants of the men who built so gloriously and created such vigorous art, live today as little better than savages in the Central American jungles. They are unaware of their heritage.

These are the cities whose discovery made headlines and whose secrets have been ferreted out by years of patient research. All have made great contributions to the store of human knowledge.

But there are many others just as fascinating, just as important, which are not nearly so well-known. They have not, as a rule, been so thoroughly investigated. Their discoverers often lacked the flamboyance and the wealth of men like Schliemann, Evans, and Thompson.

Still, their stories are no less exciting, their secrets no less mysterious, their contributions no less vital to the greater story of mankind.

It is of some of these that this book is written.

2 The Indus Valley Civilization

The early 1920's were exciting years for those interested in the science of archaeology. Not only could excavation be resumed at many sites which had been inaccessible during the long years of the first World War, but three important new discoveries were made between 1921 and 1923. Howard Carter and Lord Carnarvan caught the enthusiasm of the whole world with their discovery of the fabulous tomb of Tutankhamen, and Sir Leonard Woolley made his dramatic announcement that the Biblical Ur of the Chaldees had been found.

It was the third event, however, which was to prove one of the most startling in the entire history of archaeology. This was the discovery — in a land where few scholars even dreamed of searching for anything truly ancient — of a very old and hiterto unknown civilization!

It all began in 1921 when the Indian archaeologist, Rai Bahadur Daya Ram Sahni, dug into an intriguing mound near the village of Harappa in the Indus Valley. The site, in West Punjab, is now in Pakistan but was then part of

British India. To his surprise, among the thousands of baked-clay bricks Sahni found evidence that this site was far older than anything ever discovered in India before.

Until that moment, it had been assumed that civilized man had not made his appearance in the Indian subcontinent until around 1500 B.C. Even so early a date as that rested, not on archaeological evidence, but upon the poems of the *Rig-Veda,* which sang of how the mighty Aryan warriors had rolled over the land in their glittering chariots, destroying everything in their path. They glorified their chief god, Indra, as *puramdara* (Fort Destroyer) and credited him with the destruction of ninety such strongholds.

The oldest known site in India could be dated no earlier than the seventh or eighth centuries B.C., and certainly nothing had ever been found which remotely resembled the stone castles and hundred-walled forts Indra is supposed to have conquered. Therefore, it had long been assumed that the *Rig-Veda* exaggerated somewhat in order to make the Aryan feats of arms more heroic. There is, after all, small glory in having overrun a few tribes of ignorant savages.

The evidence which so excited the young archaeologist consisted of a number of small seal stones, beautifully engraved with pictures of animals and strange curlicues which seemed to be some unknown script.

Such seals were not entirely unknown. Sixty-five years earlier, some had fallen by accident into the hands of General Sir Alexander Cunningham, a British officer stationed in India. These seals had come to light when the railway was being constructed from Lahore to Karachi, and the mound at Harappa had, unfortunately, provided the builders with a handy supply of ballast for their roadbed.

What was more important, however, was the fact that similar— and most puzzling — seals had been found at such unlikely places as Ur and Lagash and Elam in Mesopotamia. Only recently one had turned up in the foundations of a temple of Kish, where it had apparently been thrown by accident at the time of construction. That temple had been dated in the time of King Sargon of Akkad, around 2500 B.C.!

Harappa, then, was almost certainly as old as the early civilizations in Mesopotamia. The ancient chroniclers of the *Rig-Veda* had been vindicated.

Nor was this the last of the surprises the Indus Valley had in store. In 1923, Rakhal Das Banerji of the Archaeological Survey of India dug into the foundations of a ruined Buddhist *stupa* near Mohenjo-Daro, nearly 400 miles from Harappa. He expected nothing much earlier than the third century, which was the date of the Buddhist ruins themselves. Instead he found engraved seal stones and copper amulets which were neither third century nor Buddhist. They were, in fact, exactly like those that had been found at Harappa.

Further exploration of the Indus Valley has revealed a hundred or more other sites scattered over an area twice as large as that governed by Egypt or Sumer, the other two great empires of their time. Typical artifacts of Indus manufacture have turned up almost as far south as Bombay and inland within thirty miles of New Delhi.

The Aryan invaders had, indeed, destroyed one of the greatest civilizations of ancient times. They had shattered an empire which had held the land in rigid subjugation for at least a thousand years. They had absorbed its remnants and adopted many of its accomplishments as their own. Few conquests in history have ever been more thorough. The Indus civilization vanished so completely that its very existence went unsuspected for nearly thirty-five hundred years!

As excavations progressed, it became evident that the cities of the Indus civilization were the product of one of the most strongly centralized governments the world has ever known. Despite the 400 miles — a tremendous distance for ancient times — which separate Harappa and Mohenjo-Daro, the two sites are almost identical, proving that both were planned and built by the same authority.

Not only that, but, when in the course of their thousand-year existence they fell victim to one of the terrible Indus floods, they were rebuilt on the original plan. At one site at least *nine* such rebuildings can be traced. Again we see the hand of a rigid authority, able to maintain an unchanging pattern of life for centuries.

Each of the two cities was dominated by a citadel which frowned down on the surrounding buildings from a brick platform 40 to 50 feet high. which probably served as a place of refuge in flood time. Each is a rectangle roughly 600 by 1200 feet and surrounded by baked-brick walls as much as 45 feet thick.

Within the enclosed area were a number of large public buildings, and though those at Harappa have been severely

damaged, those at Mohenjo-Daro are extremely well-pre-
served. The most striking of its structures was built
around a great tank, 39 feet long by 23 feet wide and
8 feet deep. Flights of steps lead down from the northern
and southern ends by which one might enter the water.
The treads appear to have been faced with wood or some
other material that fitted into slots at either end. The walls
and bottom were made watertight by a coating of bitumen.
An ingenious arrangement provides drainage, but the water
to fill it seems to have been carried by hand from a nearby
well.

A platform surrounds the tank, and a number of small
rooms opening from it are thought to be dressing rooms for
most authorities agree that the complex must have been
some kind of a public bath. Along a separate corridor with
a drain running down its center are eight more rooms, each
with a stairway leading up. From the thickness of the walls
it is deduced that these led not just to the roof, but to a
second floor, possibly with a gallery overlooking the tank.

Two other large buildings share space with the bath.
One, 75 by 100 feet, has walls still standing as high as
20 feet. It is believed to have been built for storage of
communal grain supplies, and it was accessible from the
river which once ran under the citadel walls. The other
measures an astonishing 78 by 230 feet and consists of a
cloistered courtyard surrounded by many cell-like rooms.
The best guess is that it was used as a place of communal
living such as a college or a convent.

What appears to have been a large columned hall may
have been a public gathering place. Other buildings with

Mohenjo-Daro in the Indus Valley, West Pakistan, revealed the existence of a hitherto-unknown civilization. The great bath shown here is believed to have religious significance.

rows of small cubicles have been identified as barracks or
storage rooms. At Harappa there were eighteen round
platforms which almost certainly served as threshing floors.

Nowhere in either city has any building been found
which could be definitely identified as either a temple or a
palace. This is a very strange omission; all other ancient
sites have at least one and commonly both. But it is quite
possible that both temple and palace do exist at Mohenjo-
Daro and are simply buried in those parts of the site which
cannot yet be excavated because they lie partly under a
Buddhist monastery. Harappa may have lost many buildings, including the two "missing" ones, to the numerous
brick takers who have raided the site.

From the base of the citadel the city proper spreads in a
gridiron pattern across the plain. Surprisingly broad streets
divide it into regular blocks each measuring 200 by 400
yards. Even when the city was living, these blocks must
have presented a peculiarly blank appearance. The solid
walls of houses, broken only by narrow windows set well
above the pavement, line either side of the street. Such
houses open only onto the narrow alleys that burrow their
way through the blocks and seem to have been deliberately
laid out to prevent the strong prevailing wind from sweep-
ing through.

Entering from this alley the visitor found himself in a
small courtyard which usually contained the household
well. The house proper was built along two sides of the
court and often had at least two stories. Some have been
found with walls still standing to a height of 35 feet, and

the existence of outside staircases suggests that each floor might have been occupied by a separate family.

Brick hearths contained the small cooking fires and supported the pottery or copper pots. The housewife used an assortment of grinders and strainers in preparing the food. She also had flint and copper knives and spoons originally made from shells but whose peculiarly lopsided design was later faithfully copied in pottery. Her pantry was usually one or more large pottery jars, which may also have served as storage space for household linens and extra clothing.

As in most ancient lands, household furnishings were few and simple — a wooden bed, a chair and table, a few stools, perhaps a chest. Floors were covered with reed mats, and light was furnished by oil lamps.

Nowhere do we find evidence of any attempts at interior decoration. No trace of architectural adornment relieves the severe utilitarianism of the Harappa cities, outside or in. Walls, though they may possibly have been plastered, are innocent of traces of the murals which so delighted other peoples. If hangings were used, of course they perished long ago.

To make up for this austerity, the citizens of Mohenjo-Daro possessed one advantage that few cities in India can boast even today: Nearly every house had an indoor bathroom with its own drainage system, and some houses had one on each floor!

A bathroom consisted of a smoothly paved floor which sloped toward one corner, where a drain was provided to carry off the water. There were also latrines with sewers for human waste. Of course, water for washing and flushing had to be brought in from the well in jars, but bathrooms seem nonetheless to have been places of enjoyment. Many pottery models, apparently toys, have been found in these bathrooms or stuck in drainpipes — forerunners of today's rubber ducks and toy boats.

Waste matter was carried through the tiled drains into the great corbel-vaulted sewers which ran under the main streets. These in turn fed into cesspools and settling tanks which were cleaned periodically by the city's scavengers. It was a very efficient system and shows engineering skills far superior to most contemporary civilizations — or many later ones, for that matter. Only the Palace of Minos at Knossos can show similar advancements, and that was only one building, not an entire city.

The lower city seems to have been divided into quarters according to occupation, where artisans and craftsmen lived, worked, and marketed their products. Here the potter deftly molded the plastic clay as it spun on the wheel or painted the distinctive black designs on the pieces before firing them. Here the weaver squatted long hours before his loom. Near the city's edge the brickmaker molded and fired thousands of brick in the two standard sizes demanded by the architects.

There is reason to believe that at least these three crafts were controlled by the government, but there were many others. Metalworkers hammered out cropper utensils and produced an occasional piece in bronze. There must have been basketmakers and carpenters and masons and all the other skilled workers that are so essential to city life.

Such were the cities of the Indus. Yet, even as they emerged slowly from the debris of centuries, the mysteries increased. It became more and more evident that they had been carefully planned before the first brick was laid. This meant that the sites were deliberately chosen, just as Americans chose the site to build Washington D.C. But why would someone choose to build a city in a spot where the temperature soars to 120 degrees in the shade and where scouring winds blow steadily across the salt crusted soil?

The answer, of course, is that no one did build in such an area.

The first clue lies in the bricks. In hot, dry climates man has always built with mud bricks dried hard in the sun. Such buildings will last for years, for centuries, as long as no moisture touches them, but they will melt and collapse in a rainy climate. Only kiln-dried bricks will stand up under repeated rains, and they are difficult and expensive to produce. Yet the cities of the Indus Valley were constructed almost entirely of kiln-dried brick.

Since man, no matter how primitive, has never been known to go to more trouble than was necessary, we must assume that the climate of the Indus Valley was different in 2500 B.C. from what it is today — in fact, quite humid and subject to tropical downpours.

There is much to support this assumption. Complicated systems of dams and dikes were constructed to control

flood waters. The elaborate drains which crisscrossed the
entire area were much too large for mere sewage lines and
must have served as storm sewers as well. They are
equipped with brick-covered manholes to allow easy access
for cleaning and repair.

Finally, the sea stones often depict animals and birds
which can no longer be found anywhere near the Indus
Valley — parrots, water buffalo, monkeys, tigers, rhinoc-
eros, elephants, all denizens of moister, less barren parts of
the subcontinent.

Why should there be this dramatic change in climate?

It has been suggested that the cities themselves were
responsible. Such tremendous building projects required
hundreds of thousands of kiln-baked bricks, which in turn
demanded tons of fuel to stoke the firing furnaces. To obtain
it the forests which once surrounded the cities were ruth-
lessly cut down, thus stripping the valley of its moisture-
retaining cover.

Another theory is that disastrous floods changed the
character of the lower valley. It is speculated that upheavals
of mud or geologic faulting might have caused periodic
dammings of the great river. Behind this natural barrier, a
lake would have formed on the plain, flooding Mohenjo-
Daro. Eventually the waters would overflow the dam site
and erode it away, draining off the lake. It is estimated that
five such great floods successively drowned the lower
Indus Valley, in the end destroying the civilization itself.

But what of the people themselves? Unfortunately we
know very little about them. They left no great body of art,
as the Egyptians did, to show us how they lived, what they

ate, how they dressed. They left no archives to tell us of their gods and rulers and heroes. We know almost nothing of their system of government and less than that of their religion. We do not even know for certain how they disposed of their dead.

Only the little seals and a few crude statuettes have survived to give us a few tantalizing hints. The seals were intended to be strung on a cord and worn around the owner's neck or wrist. They were used to seal and identify property by making an impression in clay or wax, but their subject matter was probably religious. The exquisitely carved little figures on the best of them are the highest art form known to the Indus Valley culture.

Most depict animals, and it has been suggested that these were objects of worship much like the sacred animals of ancient Egypt. A few show human figures, and some of these bear a startling resemblance to motifs of later Hindu art. One figure seated in cross-legged position and attended by a snake is particularly striking.

Compared to the seals, sculpture was extremely primitive. The great bulk of the finds has been small clay or pottery figurines, though one haughty-looking and extremely lifelike dancing girl is done in bronze. Terra-cotta animals are generally much more skillfully executed. Stone was little used, but some examples have been found, of which the best done is the head of a bearded man.

The fact that the statuettes are nearly all of women has led some scholars to believe that here was another center of worship of the great mother-goddess which was so common throughout the ancient world.

The lack of palaces or monumental statues dedicated to individual rulers — coupled with the absence of rich, ceremonial burials — seems to argue a political organization headed by some kind of committee. If so, it was a powerful one, able to regulate the smallest details of everyday life.

Dress seems to have been quite simple and suited to a hot, humid climate Women apparently wore only a cotton skirt with many necklaces and bracelets. Men contented themselves with wrapping a length of cloth about their loins and adding a shawl, worn in Roman-toga fashion, for more formal occasions. Both sexes made up for any plainness of attire by adding jewelry. Ornaments of copper, silver, gold, and polished gemstones were worn in great profusion. A special quarter of the city was devoted to the craftsmen who produced such baubles.

Female hairstyles were quite elaborate and headdresses even more so — some high and fan-shaped, others with horns or great flapping earpieces. A few had little pannier-like baskets on either side which may have served to hold burning incense.

Women were not without their little vanities even in those days; as evidence many ivory combs, charcoal pencils, and metal mirrors were found among the ruins. Hundreds of small boxes with tight-fitting lids point to the widespread use of cosmetics and scented oils. Copper or bronze rods about 5 inches long were probably used to apply kohl to the eyelids.

A familiar note is added by the array of children's toys which have been discovered. Marbles and rattles abound, as do dice and maze games and bird-shaped whistles. There were many toy animals — some with wheels, others with heads that could be made to nod by pulling a string. There was even a perfect little model of a two-wheeled cart complete with draft animals to pull it. Tiny terra-cotta cages may once have held small animals or even pet insects. Some model animals appear to be the work of children and even carry tiny fingerprints baked into the clay.

Such farming implements as have been found are exceedingly primitive. Still, we know that they managed to cultivate several grains — which were stored in the government granaries or in large pit silos— as well as melons, peas, and possibly dates. A tiny fragment of cotton fabric, preserved by being embedded in the oxide of a silver jar, affords proof that these people were the first in the world to cultivate the valuable cotton plant. Domesticated animals included humped cattle and water buffalo, and probably horses, asses, camels — possibly even pigs.

As nearly as can be told from the fragments of art and the skeletal remains, there were two distinct racial types living in the cities of the Indus. One was of medium size with dark skin and hair, long head, and narrow prominent nose. People of this type may still be found living in Northwest India. The second race were small men with black hair, broad faces, wide noses, and thick lips. They resembled the people still living in Southern India.

Was one group a ruling class, holding the others in subjection? Or did the two races live together in equality? Again, we do not know, although in the light of present knowledge, the former seems more probable.

Archaeologists do not believe that the Harappan culture

actually developed in the Indus Valley. It simply appeared there, more or less perfected, somewhere around 2500 B.C. This would tend to support the theory that one of the two facial types was the invader who brought his civilization with him. But where did these people come from?

Though this is little more than speculation, it seems most likely that they migrated from the eastern mountain valleys of Iran, beginning about 3000 B.C. Preliminary investigation of sites along the route they must have taken are encouraging. Tentatively, then, we may identify the Indus Valley settlers as hill people who already possessed bronze tools and weapons and possibly a slight knowledge of the Mesopotamian cities to the west.

The Harappans were in contact with Sumer, and traded extensively with Mesopotamia and beyond — to Troy, perhaps even to Knossos. Spectrographic analysis has proved that the composition of a pair of similar beads — one found at Harappa, the other on Crete — is identical. Obviously they had a common source. Seals and other small items of Indus origin have been found in Mesopotamia, and a few cylinder seals from Sumer, animal-headed pins, gold beads, and the like from scattered sites in the Near East have been recovered along the Indus.

Such objects as beads, however, are assumed to have been incidental to a more thriving exchange, probably in perishable goods. Woven cloth has been suggested — perhaps the cotton cloth already known in the Indus Valley — or even slaves.

A necessity for almost any type of commerce is an established system of weights and measures, and in these things the Indus sites are rich. An astonishing number of extremely accurate weights has been recovered, along with many examples of the simple balance scales in which they were used. The Indus people seem to have employed both binary and decimal systems, for the smaller weights are graduated in units of two, the larger in units of ten. Nor are standards of linear measurement lacking. Ten small units apparently made up a standard "foot" of 13.2 inches, and there was also a unit corresponding to the Egyptian cubit, 20.7 inches.

The Island of Bahrein in the Persian Gulf may have been the trading center referred to by the Sumerians, through which they exchanged goods with a mysterious people called *Meluhha*. These may or may not have been the *Mleccha* whom the Vedas say the Aryans destroyed in India, but certain finds on the island indicate that it had contact both with Mesopotamia and the Indus Valley. Perhaps thorough excavation of Bahrein's thousands of burial tumuli will afford proof.

How the archaeologists, who have to sift through tons of earth to locate even tiny, elusive bits of evidence, must sigh when they turn up still another carved seal or bit of inscribed pottery. How tantalizing to know that the solution to many a mystery might be in their hands — if only they could read it!

Unfortunately, whatever archives or commercial accounts the Indus people kept must have been written on some perishable material which has vanished without a trace. All that remain are the seals and amulets and a few potsherds. Of these, the seals are by far the most numerous, yet each of them contains an average of only six signs. Estimates of the total number of separate characters range from 253 to nearly 400. Either one would give us far too many for an alphabetic system of writing and not nearly enough for a purely pictorial one. In all probability, the Harappan script, like that of ancient Egypt, was a combination phonetic-pictographic one.

So far, all attempts to decipher the mysterious glyphs have ended in failure. We can only conclude, along with Sir Mortimer Wheeler, that "the script bears no ascertainable relationship with any contemporary or near-contemporary script."

The extreme difficulty of the task has not kept the linguists from trying, and some suggestions have shown originality, to say the least. Bedrich Hrozny, a Czechoslovakian scholar who had brilliantly deciphered Hittite script, tried to prove a tie between the Harappans and Hittite, and there was even a serious school of thought which equated the Indus inscriptions to the kohau *rongo rongo*, or "talking board," script of far-off Easter Island. But linguists dismiss this contention as highly improbable.

Science's best hope of decipherment lies in the possibility that somewhere there exists a bilingual inscription, like that of the Rosetta stone, which would give linguists the key. Such an inscription may turn up tomorrow — or a century from now. Perhaps it does not exist. Meanwhile, linguists continue to study each new inscription in the hope that it may provide the clue which will unravel the mysteries of the Indus Valley and tell us how it all began.

We need no script, no history books, to tell us how it

ended, at least not for Mohenjo-Daro. The death throes of that city are recorded all too clearly in the unmistakable evidence of its ruins.

There is some indication that the power of the central government had been declining for some time, possibly strangled by its own rigid inability to adapt to a changing environment. At any rate, the cold perfection is missing from the newest building projects, and the latest repairs are more than a little slipshod. Artistry declines, and the people grow poorer and poorer, perhaps from the devastation of floods.

So the power that had lasted for a thousand years began to waver, to give way under pressure from the Aryan hordes that prowled its borders.

These Aryans, possibly closely related to those who were moving into Asia Minor and Greece at about the same time, seem to have originated at the southern slopes of the Himalayas. They were a fierce semi-nomadic people who spoke an Indo-European language and almost certainly possessed the lightweight war chariot which made them such formidable foes. At first, they may have contented themselves with raids, and such forays could have taken place for many years.

Then, about 1500 B.C., the pressure of other waves of barbarians moving in behind forced them forward. They must now conquer or perish, and that is never a hard decision to make.

It is difficult to see how a city so strong and well organized as Mohenjo-Daro could have been taken by surprise, but that is apparently what happened. Every sign points to the fact that the appearance of barbarians in those broad streets was as sudden as it was unexpected.

To be sure, the Indus people do not seem to have been accustomed to warfare. Surprisingly few weapons have been discovered in the ruins, and aside from the citadels, they apparently constructed no defensive works. For ten centuries they had lived in peace, their only enemy the river at their doorstep.

Now, the Aryans stormed through the defenseless city like avenging demons, killing its citizens wherever they found them. In the streets, in the shops, in their homes, in public places and private, men, women, and children died under the weapons of the invaders.

And then the looting began — looting that started with gold and jewels and ended up with the theft of an entire civilization. When they had seized whatever they wanted, the Aryan conquerors simply marched away, leaving the ruined city behind, not even bothering to occupy it. Apparently they were not yet civilized enough to realize the advantages of city living, for none of the cities was ever lived in again, once the Indus people disappeared. Perhaps it was superstitious fear which kept the Aryans from venturing into those silent streets.

For Mohenjo-Daro was not only a dead city; it was, as its native name says, a "Place of the Dead." No one even bothered to bury the victims of that last terrible raid. They lay just as they had fallen, and their once-powerful city became their only tomb.

The river, unchecked now by the crumbling dikes, flowed through the empty streets. Year after year, century after century, it brought its annual load of silt down from the mountains, until the city and its grim occupants were hidden from view.

They were still there thirty-four hundred years later when the spades of the excavators gently stripped away the layers of silt and found them. The last citizens of Mohenjo-Daro lay alone in the terrible solitude of death or littered the narrow alleys in pitiful little groups. Thirteen skeletons were found in one room alone, and in another group of nine, five were those of young children. Some had been decapitated as they ran through the streets seeking refuge.

And so they died, and with their death the curtain of Indian history closes for twelve centuries until Alexander the Great crossed the Indus to find a flourishing civilization in 325 B.C.

Only now we know that that civilization did not spring up spontaneously like a desert flower. Instead, its roots were thrust deep into the past — and the seed from which they sprang was planted long ago in the silent cities of the Indus.

3 *The Sacred City of the Aten*

The towering pyramids and massive temples of Egypt had never been lost. Their decaying splendor was ever a source of wonder to the ancients themselves. Early travelers, like the Greek Herodotus, though they viewed them many centuries before Christ, were as impressed with their majesty and antiquity as any modern tourist.

However, it was not until the eighteenth century of our era that the study of these incredibly old Egyptian monuments gave birth to a new science — archaeology. When Napoleon Bonaparte made his famous invasion of the Nile kingdom in 1798, he took with him not only a force of thirty-eight thousand soldiers, but a smaller army composed of 175 of France's most learned men. The soldiers accomplished their mission of conquest, but their success was fleeting. The scientists made only a small beginning on theirs, which was to study and record the mysterious ruins. But the work they began is still going on.

It took years of study, twenty-four volumes of text, and twelve volumes of plates for the French scientists to publish their findings. More important, they returned with a strange bilingual stone which trench-digging soldiers had uncovered at the little village of Rosetta. It proved to be the key which would unlock the mysteries of Egyptian hieroglyphics.

As time went by, the history of the ancient land began to take form like the fitting together of an enormously complex puzzle. But here and there were pieces which simply could not be fit in anywhere. Baffling references, like that of the inscription at Mes, to "the criminal of Akhetaten" or "the heretic king" cropped up. But where were the monuments of such a king? Nobody knew.

Then, one day in 1887, a peasant woman knelt in the blazing sun and scraped away the deep sand on the eastern bank of the Nile. She was digging for *sebakh,* a rich, nitrous soil which was much valued as fertilizer by the farmers of the area, but she did not find it. Instead, her fingers encountered hard objects beneath the sandy wastes — baked-clay tablets covered with strange marks.

The woman can hardly have been surprised at such a discovery. The land of Egypt has been described as nothing but "one vast cemetery," and its soil is studded with mementos of its glorious past. Nor was she disappointed in her find. Like every other Egyptian, she knew that the foreigners prowled the land like hungry beasts in search of just such useless trash as this. And they were silly enough to pay enormous prices for it. In fact, some of her people had become amazingly skillful at manufacturing 'antiquities" for the tourist trade.

Carelessly, she crammed the fragile earthen slabs into her

sacks and lugged them off to a dealer of such objects in the
city of Luxor. What could it matter if some of them were
broken to bits or ground to powder by such rough treat-
ment? After all, there were plenty of them.

It seemed to matter even less when the first French
scholar to examine the find pronounced the tablets nothing
but forgeries. The head of the Egyptian Antiquities Service
did even worse. He simply ignored them, and many more
were damaged by careless handling and storage before
anyone was curious enough to examine them again.

When at last it was realized that these bits of hardened
mud were not only genuine, but that they came from the
archives of an Eighteenth Dynasty Pharoah, only 350 of the
priceless documents were still in readable condition. The
tablets were written in cuneiform Akkadian, a diplomatic
language of the time, and could be read easily. They turned
out to be "letters" between Egyptian officials and the
governments of such contemporary civilizations as Babylon,
Assyria, Phoenicia, and the Hittites.

Needless to say, the deciphering of these tablets caused a
sensation in archaeological circles and a burning desire to
dig at the site of their discovery.

In 1891 Sir Flinders Petrie, one of the greatest Egyptol-
ogists, began excavations near the village of Tell el Amarna,
nearly 200 miles down the Nile from ancient Thebes. Almost
at once he was rewarded with exciting but puzzling discoveries.

The magnificent fresco which now adorns Britain's
Ashmolean Museum is one. It reveals, along with many
others, a new concept in Egyptian art. Gone are the stiff,

stylized figures of the tombs and temples. Realistic animals lurk among realistic foliage. Waterfowl fly up from papyrus reeds so true to life one can almost hear the whir of their wings. Flowers bloom, and waters ripple, and silvery fish swim lazily beneath the surface of those waters. And the men and women who appear in these scenes are portrayed with the same grace and freedom of movement.

Truly the artists of the city, which was gradually emerging from three thousand years beneath the sands, had held an undistorted mirror to life for the first time in history. The result was like a fresh breeze blowing through musty corridors.

Petrie discovered one such masterpiece painted on the pavement of one of the ruined courtyards. To preserve its glowing colors and delicate lines from destruction seemed an impossible task until he hit upon an ingenious plan. Lying flat on a low scaffold, the archaeologist painstakingly coated every square inch of that fragile surface with a thin layer of cooked tapioca. He was forced to work very carefully, using only his fingers to spread the sticky stuff, for even the softest brush tended to flake off the powdery pigments.

Petrie then caused a raised walkway to be built over the courtyard so that visitors might view it without the possibility of damage from a careless foot. Alas! The very beauty of the pavement proved the cause of its destruction.

The droves of tourists who came to marvel at the consummate artistry displayed there heedlessly trampled down the crops of the neighboring fields. This so enraged the farmer that in retaliation he chopped the priceless work of art to pieces. Today all that remains of the masterpiece are Petrie's carefully executed drawings and one fragment which he was able to raise intact. These are now in the British Museum, where they provide a tantalizing glimpse of the magnificence of the lost original.

But paintings and murals were not all that Tell el Amarna had to offer. Petrie and his successors have excavated the ruins of temples, palaces, halls, courts, mansions, and even what might have been a zoological garden. The royal pleasure palace, located in the north suburb, contained a lovely suite of rooms for the Pharaoh. It consisted of a retiring room with a dais for the throne, a bedroom and a bath, all arranged about a small private courtyard. The cellars of the palace have yielded clay seals announcing that they once contained wine for the King's table, "a very good wine."

Aside from the buildings themselves, finds have ranged from ring bezels and beads made of faience (glazed clay) and tweezers, needles, fishhooks, scissors, and amulets of bronze — to hoards of gold and silver and many more fabulous works of art. One portrait bust discovered by the German expedition of 1907-1914 is probably worth more than the combined costs of all the expeditions to date.

The bust shows the small head of a woman poised gracefully and regally atop a slender, curving neck. The delicate features are perfectly chiseled, the inlaid eyes large and compellingly lovely. This bust has been acclaimed, and justly so, both as a masterpiece of the sculptor's art and as a classic example of surpassing feminine beauty. It depicts Nefertiti, the Queen.

This head of Nefertiti, Queen of Egypt, mother-in-law of Tutankhamen was discovered in the ruins of Tell el Amarna, site of the long-lost capitol of Akhenaten.

Even the lesser finds exhibit a striking degree of artistry. Picture, if you can, the glowing splendor of the necklace of glazed clay beads described in the following words of an archaeologist's report:

1 row small cornflowers, blue and green
1 row poppy leaves
1 row bunches of grapes, blue
1 row white-flower petals with yellow bases and one-
    inch long cornflowers, blue with green stems
1 row dates — 2 red, 1 green, 2 blue, 1 green, 2 red, etc.
1 row lotus petals, blue tips

It is not difficult to imagine how such an ornament must have shimmered, how its colors must have blazed against the snowy linen garments of its long-dead owner.

But who was that owner? Who commissioned artist and artisan to fly in the face of long-established traditions and produce such masterpieces? Who lived in these palaces and worshipped in these temples? Above all, who sat on the throne of the Pharaohs so far from the royal city of Thebes?

The man and his city have emerged together from the mists of time.

His name was Amenhotep IV, and he has been described by historian James Henry Breasted as "the world's first idealist and the world's first *individual*." Amenhotep IV was apparently the first man ever to conceive and establish the worship of a single, all-powerful god. His story is the story of Egypt's forgotten city.

In 1375 B.C. Amenhotep had inherited from his father, Amenhotep III, a far-flung military empire whose peoples paid homage to literally hundreds of gods. The most important of these was Amen-Ra, god of Thebes, whose priests were wealthy and powerful enough to exert a great influence on the throne itself. On more than one occasion they had even chosen the man who sat on that throne.

But the young Amenhotep preferred to worship the god Aten, personification of the beneficial aspects of the sun. Almost as soon as he gained the throne, the new Pharaoh broke with the mighty priesthood of Amen, forbade the worship of Amen, destroyed his temples, and declared Aten as the only true god in Egypt.

To make the break more dramatic, he changed his name from Amenhotep (Amen Rests) to Akhenaten (Spirit of Aten). Nor did he stop there. At a place far from Thebes, where the eastern hills draw away from the Nile to leave a crescent of open land, he set up the four great boundary stones which would mark the site of a new capital city. It would be a holy city, completely unlike the Amen-dominated capital of his fathers.

In honor of his god he called the city Akhetaten (The Horizon of Aten). It was the official archives of Akhetaten which yielded the important correspondence known to science as the Tell el Amarna letters.

Soon the hills echoed to the sounds of frenzied construction, and great buildings began to rise from the barren sands. Within a short space of two years, the new city was complete. Now gracious palaces and magnificent temples, surrounded by luxurious gardens, cast their cool green-and-white reflections across the waters of the Nile. Here the

Pharaoh and his family took up residence, delighting in freedom from formality, living openly and naturally before their people.

The Pharaoh's way of life may have been the inspiration for the new concept in art which adorned the city. His chief sculptor, Bek, includes among his many titles the phrase "whom His Majesty himself taught." This seems to indicate that Akhenaten's teachings of "living in truth" inspired the naturalism and freedom of Tell el Amarna art.

What an exciting moment it must have been when the royal couple first stepped ashore at their shining new city! The royal barge, *The Aten Gleams,* dropped anchor beside the newly built quay, and the Lord of Upper and Lower Egypt, his Queen, their family and friends stepped ashore to take up their new lives in the glittering new city. How the crowds must have cheered as the royal pair entered the waiting chariot to be borne away along the wide avenues to the luxurious palace.

Perhaps the Pharaoh even took the reins himself, as he seems to have done quite often, and embraced his lovely consort as he guided the horses through the crowd. They are shown thus in one of the surviving murals. With them in the chariot is their royal daughter, Meritaten (Beloved of Aten). The mischievous little princess is shown leaning over the railing of the chariot as she playfully pokes at the horses' flanks with her stick.

For a time Akhenaten, living son of the living Aten, seemed to be the most fortunate of mortals. He was married to a beautiful queen The lovely sculptured bust discovered

by the Germans is a portrait of his wife — Nefertiti (The
Beautiful Lady Has Come).

This graceful Queen seems to have been as good as she
was beautiful. Many inscriptions sing the praises of her
kindness, her generosity, her charm. She was also a devout
worshiper of Aten, setting even the Pharaoh an example by
her piety.

Akhenaten and Nefertiti had no son. Over the years, five
more little princesses joined Meritaten in the royal nurseries,
but never a prince. The little girls were given the tongue-
twisting names of Meketaten, Ankhsenpaaten, Nefer-
nefreu-Aten, Neferneferkure and Setepenre, and their illus-
trious parents seem to have lavished affection on them. If
the King and Queen sorrowed over the lack of a son, it is
not apparent.

The worship of Aten was apparently bright and joyous.
Festivals and religious celebrations filled the new city with
song and laughter. Temples were open to the heavens so
that the sun, symbolized by his disk, the Aten, might shed
his purifying light on all that took place within them. No
bloody sacrifices stained his altars; no dark mysteries
attended his rites. Nothing but hymns of praise, offerings of
fruit and garlanded flowers, and clouds of perfumed incense
were demanded of Aten worshipers, who hailed their god
as "Bringer of Life."

Large portions of two hymns to Aten, presumably composed by Akhenaten himself, have survived to give us an
idea of what the new religion was like. Not only are they
fine enough to be classed as literature, but they may have

been the inspiration for some of the poetic passages in the Bible. For example the following passage:

O lord, how manifold are thy works!
While thou wast alone:
O thou sole god, whose powers no other possesseth,
Thou didst create the earth according to thy desire.
Men, all cattle large and small,
All that go upon the earth,
That go about upon their feet;
All that are on high,
That fly with their wings.
The countries of Syria and Nubia,
The land of Egypt;
Thou settest every man in his place,
Thou suppliest their necessities.
Every one has his possessions,
And his days are reckoned.

To this poet-king, the world, of which he had been given such a large segment as "his possessions," was of little importance. His chief interest in the colonial possessions of Egypt seems to have been a desire to establish the worship of his god among their people. In this he was only mildly successful, but in far-off Nubia the ruins of a temple to The Living Aten still stands. For the most part, Akhenaten preferred to worship his god and dream his dreams, far removed from the scenes of civil strife and deaf to the needs of his people for a strong monarch.

Unfortunately, few of Akhenaten's subjects ever really understood their dreaming monarch or his strange god. But they could easily see that piety was no substitute for good government. Under Akhenaten's weak rule, the outlawed priests of Amen began to plot, the conquered nations began to rebel, and traitors began to appear even among the King's most trusted servants. As the gentle Pharaoh composed his hymns, the mighty empire he had inherited from his father was melting away like snow in the bright light of the Aten.

The Tell el Amarna letters include official dispatches from all over the world, many of them urgent pleas for the Pharaoh to send military aid to hold the crumbling empire together. One faithful vassal wrote sixty letters in a frantic effort to persuade Akhenaten to send troops to put down a rebellion in his province. Another wrote, "And now, Tunip, thy city, weeps, and her tears are flowing, and there is no help for us. For twenty years we have been sending to our lord the king, the king of Egypt, but there has not come to us a word, no, not one!"

Like the unfortunate lord of Tunip, they all pleaded in vain.

It has been suggested that Akhenaten never saw the letters, and such a theory is not without some justification. One letter from the known traitor, Airu, to the King's trusted foreign minister, Tutu, indicates that treachery was present in very high places.

Still, the king must have noticed that the flow of gold and ivory and slaves — all the varied wealth with which the subject nations had paid tribute to mighty Egypt — had dwindled to a trickle. He must have known that the hated priesthood of Amen, whose very name he had outlawed, was gaining power with every passing day. He must have

known that the once flourishing trade of Egypt was at a
standstill, that the crops had been meager for several
seasons, and that the starving people were cursing the
names of Akhenaten and his god throughout the land.

Too late the visionary Pharaoh awakened from his dream.
He raised Smenkhkare husband of Princess Meritaten, to
the throne beside him and, as a sop to the people and
priests, even sent the young couple to rule from Thebes. He
himself refused to leave his beloved city of Akhetaten.

But the golden peace he had sought was forever
shattered. The death of his second-born daughter, Meketaten, left the royal father bowed with grief. Then came
the crowning blow. Nefertiti, perhaps angered at the com-
promise with the priests of Amen, either left her husband or
rebelled against him and was banished. She retired to the
northern suburb, taking the King's young half-brother,
Tutankhaten, with her.

Now the light of the sacred sun disk seemed to flicker
and fade about the desolate King. In the seventeenth year
of his reign, the forty-first of his short life, Akhenaten
sickened and died. With the untimely death of Smenkhkare
soon afterward, the throne fell to Tutankhaten, now
married to Princess Ankhsenpaaten. Perhaps the boy clung
to Aten worship for a while under the guidance of Nefertiti,
but he was soon under the thumb of the Amen priesthood.
This is obvious from the fact that he changed his name to
Tutankh*amen.*

The city of light did not long survive its founder. Its
streets were soon deserted; its gardens shriveled and died
for lack of care. The vengeful priests defaced its murals and

monuments in their efforts to erase every trace of their old enemy. Even carved inscriptions were chiseled away. The palaces and temples were used as quarries for magnificent new monuments to the triumphant god of Thebes.

Finally, the sands of the desert crept slowly back to collapse roofs and topple walls and, when the work of destruction was complete, to give a decent burial to the mangled remains.

As the centuries passed, the hated name of Akhetaten was erased from the pages of history as thoroughly as it had been from the inscriptions. Now, thanks to archaeology, the city and its founder live once more.

About 4 miles up along a narrow, rock-walled wadi which cuts its way into the eastern hills lie the forgotten tombs of the Aten worshipers. It is here that we can meet once more the people of Akhetaten and see them as they were in the fleeting days of their city's glory.

Few of the tombs were ever really completed. Fewer still were occupied by their builders. All show signs of hasty construction. Everywhere there are quotations from the hymns to Aten and frequently his symbol. This is a disk with long rays reaching down and terminating in little hands which seem to caress the Pharaoh who was his living son.

Even the royal tomb was left unfinished, and it has been described as grim and depressing. Here, a sloping passageway leads downward to a flight of steps steeply cut into the living rock and ending in the empty burial chamber. Beyond lies a hall where murals once showed the royal family worshiping their god, but these have been deliberately and severely damaged. At the top of the stairs a short side passage leads to the burial chamber of the little princess Meketaten, though there is no sign of her body.

It is, indeed, a mournful spot.

On other tombs, less a target for the fury of Amen, there are reliefs and murals of surpassing beauty, in which the royal family may be seen in the happier moments when the Aten smiled. The tomb of Minister Tutu, for example, shows a radiant Nefertiti sitting with two of her daughters on her knees while Akhenaten confers "exceptional reward" on his courtier.

On the walls of the tomb of the chief of police, Mahu, the King and Queen drive forth in a golden chariot. Mahu and fifteen of his force run alongside. The chief seems to be everywhere. He is in the crowd which waves good-bye to the royal pair, and he stands once more at the head of the delegation awaiting them at their destination.

Still another tomb, that of Ay, one of the Pharaoh's principal ministers, give mute testimony to the haste with which construction was abandoned. It was planned on a scale only slightly less grand than that of the King. Only fifteen of its twenty-four columns stand complete, and its murals are unfinished. Still, there are several glimpses of life in Akhetaten.

On one wall the ladies of Ay's household amuse themselves by dancing or playing harps and lutes or arranging one another's hair in the latest fashion. On another we see Akhenaten standing on a balcony accompanied by his wife and three of the ever-present princesses. All are literally showering golden ornaments, vessels, collars, and rings on the delighted Ay, who stands in the courtyard below with his wife. Both have hands upraised to catch the golden shower. In the background dozens of servants caper and bow their thanks for the signal honor being done their master, while scribes record the loot and chariots stand ready to haul it away.

The tomb of Huya, a high official in the Queen Mother's household, records a state visit made by Queen Tiyi to her son. The scene depicted is a family dinner presided over by Akhenaten who lounges comfortably, gnawing on a bone. On the left is Nefertiti, two daughters in low chairs at her side. The Queen holds an entire roast fowl in her hands with surprising grace. On the right is Queen Tiyi. She too has a princess at her side, and she is pictured in the act of offering the child some tidbit. Each of the adults has his own table groaning with tempting delicacies, while enormous wine jars stand nearby to quench the royal thirst.

Never before had the royal occupant of a throne been portrayed with such revealing informality. But then, there had never before been a King such as Akhenaten. And never before had there been such a dream.

The dust of battle rose to obscure the delicate colors of that dream. Cries of vengeance and the clash of arms drowned out the gentle hymns raised to the glory of the Aten. The sweet scent of incense was overpowered by the smell of death, and the flowery garlands shriveled on the deserted altars. The world was not yet ready to accept a religion of peace.

4 The Land of Hatti

Asia Minor stretches westward from Asia proper to form a natural land bridge between the Black and Mediterranean Seas. Since the beginning of history, this area has served as a highway over which men, materials, and ideas have passed back and forth between the eastern and western worlds. The long-settled coastal lands are fertile and inviting, but in the center of modern Turkey the land rises steeply, and tortuous mountain chains swirl in a craggy circle to surround and isolate the Anatolian Plateau.

The rugged and inaccessible area enclosed by those forbidding heights is certainly no earthly paradise. The soil is generally poor, and extremes of temperature severely limit the crops which can be grown in even the most fertile valleys. It would be hard to imagine a more inhospitable land or one so poorly suited to be the home of one of the ancient world's most powerful civilizations. Perhaps that is why the secrets of Anatolia remained so long hidden while scientists searched other places in vain.

But in 1812 a Swiss travel writer named Johann Ludwig

Burckhardt, reported having seen a peculiarly inscribed stone at a town called Hamath in Syria. Thereafter, from time to time, more of these "Hamath stones" turned up in other places. Many were found in Syria, others in Anatolia, Turkey. All apparently had a common origin, but no one could guess what it was, and the mysterious inscriptions defied all efforts at translation.

In 1834, Charles Felix Marie Texier journeyed to the Anatolian plateau to investigate what he believed to be the remains of a Graeco-Roman settlement called Tavium. Near the modern Turkish village of Boghazköy he was amazed to discover the massive ruins of a great walled city. The "grandeur and peculiar nature of the ruins," set so unexpectedly in so desolate a spot, convinced Texier that, whoever had built them, it was not the Romans.

The ruins at Boghazköy lie above the village on a rocky spur of land which rises sharply from the valley floor. Two streams meet just below this spot after cutting deep gorges on either hand. On this commanding height, walls over 4 miles in length enclose an area of approximately 300 acres.

At least five temples have been excavated within these walls. The largest measure roughly 50 to 70 feet, not counting its sprawling complex of storehouses, courtyards, and colonnades. The walls of this imposing structure are as much as 3 feet thick, and the lower courses consist of stones over 6 feet long. It is paved with colossal slabs of limestone carefully dressed to form a curved joint with the walls. The other temples, though smaller, have roughly the same floor plan and construction.

Aside from the defensive works and the temples, little has survived but two groups of rectangular storage chambers but these, as we shall see, proved the most important finds of all.

As if all this were not enough, a native guide proudly led the wondering Frenchman some two miles out from the village to point out one of the local landmarks. It involved a gruelling climb into the towering cliffs 600 feet above the valley floor, but it was well worth it. Texier was undoubtedly the first European ever to set eyes on the place the villagers called the Yazilikaya — (The Inscribed Rock).

There, where a deep gorge sliced its way into the cliffs, a series of galleries and grottoes penetrated far back into the limestone to form what can only have been an ancient shrine. Along the walls on either side ran a band of sculptured reliefs—badly worn by centuries of exposure to the elements but still clearly recognizable as a series of individual figures.

More than sixty strong, they marched in solemn procession down the ever-narrowing cleft to meet where an isolated rock faced toward the entrance to the largest gallery. Here the two principal figures stood confronting each other above a stone shelf which may once have supported an altar. The figure on one side, it was later learned, was the mighty storm god, Teshub, accompanied by his sacred bulls and standing atop his symbolic mountain. On the other was the sun goddess Hebat or Wurusemu, surrounded by her own symbols.

To the right of this group was a narrow cleft leading to

an inner sanctuary and guarded by grotesquely carved figures. Here were more reliefs, including one which was later identified as King Tudhaliyas IV being embraced by the so-called Young God. His likeness on the walls now serves to date the shrine at about 1250 B.C.

Despite their interest these marvelous carvings were not in themselves nearly so important as the inscriptions which were interspersed among them. For here again were the tantalizing Hamath-stone inscriptions. Unfortunately, Texier failed to recognize them, and a vital clue was missed.

Meanwhile, scholars were busily working at the enigma presented by the stones. Among the most diligent was Archibald Henry Sayce, an Oxford professor who has been referred to as "the High Priest of the Hittites."

Assuming that a people who had left such widespread evidence could not have gone completely unnoticed by their contemporaries, he searched the writings of the ancients for clues. He found several very interesting items. For one thing, Egyptian troops under Rameses II had fought the famous battle of Kadesh against an enemy they referred to as "the abominable Kheta," and a treaty was signed between the two lands in 1269 B.C. For another, Assyrian records of 1100 B.C. speak of Syria as "the Land of Hatti."

Finally, the Hebrew chroniclers of the Old Testament often mentioned a people called "the Hittites." For example, in both the books of Genesis and Joshua, the Lord sends the Israelites into "the land of the Hittites." Esau and Solomon both took wives from among them, and Solomon seems to have negotiated with their king. The book of Numbers tells us flatly that they "dwell in the mountains."

Some of these Biblical references are hard to explain, since, as far as we know, the Hittites never came nearer to Palestine than Damascus.

But Sayce had no way of knowing this, and, in a series of brilliant deductions, he leaped to the conclusion that the Kheta of the Egyptians, the Hatti of the Assyrians, and the Hittites of the Hebrews were one and the same people and that they were responsible for the inscriptions.

"It was clear," he wrote in his *Reminiscences,* "that in pre-Hellenic days a powerful empire must have existed in Asia Minor— and possessed its own special artistic culture and its own special script. And so the story of the Hittite Empire was introduced to the world."

It was not quite so simple as all that. Sayce published his theory in 1879, but it was not accepted with wild enthusiasm. Most scholars regarded it as interesting but incapable of proof. A few even indulged in jests at his expense, accusing him flatly of inventing his Hittites.

And then the Tell el Amarna letters were found. Those priceless documents went far to prove that Sayce had been right on almost every count. Only in his guess that Hittite civilization had originated in Syria was he discredited. The letters definitely spoke of their conquest of that land.

So the Hittites were real, and the Hamath inscriptions were undoubtedly theirs. Still the mystery was far from a solution, for no one knew where the conquerers had come from. Nor could all the Tell el Amarna letters be read. Some were written in a strange language and addressed to a king of Arzawa. Could this belong to the Hittites? Again, no one knew.

So matters stood until the French archaeologist, Ernest Chantre, discovered fragments of similar tablets at the site of Texier's unidentified city in Anatolia. Immediately every interested scholar, including Sayce himself, was clamoring to excavate at Boghazköy. But the coveted concession was awarded to a German expedition under Assyriologist Dr. Hugo Winckler, who began to dig in 1906.

Needless to say, Winckler's operation and methods were subject to close scrutiny — and almost universal criticism — from the disappointed candidates. Sayce contemptuously referred to his colleague as an architect rather than an archaeologist and complained that "even the sequence of pottery is uncertain."

Not all the complaints can be ascribed to jealousy. Winckler does seem to have been much more interested in the tablets his workmen brought him than in the irksome task of supervising those workmen at the dig. His own countryman, the classical scholar Emil Curtius, was appalled to see one digger snatching the precious clay tablets from the earth "like a peasant woman digging potatoes."

For the unimpressive "storerooms" at Boghazköy had yielded a treasure trove of cuneiform tablets, preserved through the centuries in amazingly orderly rows. Many were in the easily read Akkadian and proved to be the counterpart of the Tell el Amarna letters — "the diplomatic correspondence of a people who called themselves Hatti — and the site could be definitely identified as their capital city, Hattusas.

In August of 1916, a discovery was made which sent the

phlegmatic Winckler into almost poetic ecstasy. "One glance," he wrote, "and all my life's experiences crumbled into insignificance. Here it was — something I might in jest have thought of as a fairy's gift." One can almost feel the excitement with which he spelled out the text, which concerned the well-known treaty between Rameses II and a Hittite king, and which was identical, word for word, with certain paragraphs of the treaty !

In all, over ten thousand of the baked-clay tablets were rescued from their long oblivion. Many were in the same unknown language that had first appeared at Tell el Amarna, but enough were written in Akkadian to furnish a fairly connected history of the Hittite Empire from 1350 to 1210 B.C. and tantalizing glimpses of the earlier periods. The wide gaps might be filled in if only the Hamath hieroglyphs and the "Arzawa" cuneiform could be deciphered.

Many had tried to solve the riddles. Sayce had failed in 1880, and his successors had no better luck. In 1902, a Norwegian philologist, J. A. Knudtzon, ventured the opinion that they were not dealing with an Indo-European language. He suffered such ridicule at the hands of his learned colleagues that he was forced to back down, and another dozen years passed with progress.

It remained for a Czech, Bedrich Hrozny, to find the key to the puzzle and prove that poor Knudtzon had been right after all. Already eminent in the fields of Assyriology and linguistics, Hrozny began his study of Hittite in 1911. Despite the interruptions of World War I, he was able to publish his "Solution to the Hittite Problem" in 1915.

Though the hieroglyphs which had started the whole thing had to wait until bilingual inscriptions were discovered in 1945, most of the Boghazköy cuneiform texts could be read with considerable accuracy by 1917.

The tablets, it turned out, were written in *eight* different languages. In addition to Akkadian and Sumerian and the recently deciphered Hittite, the archives contained texts in Luvian, Palaic, Mittanian, and non-Indo-European Hurrian. The eighth language was the most confusing. It was another non-Indo-European tongue called Hattite — and Hattite, not Hittite, seems to have been the native language of the Hittites!

Confusing? Yes, but now that the evidence has been sifted, it is fairly clear what happened. Sometime between 3000 and 2000 B.C., there lived in the land of Hatti a people who spoke Hattite and built Hattusas as their capital. Then came invaders from the north to overrun and conquer the land of Hatti. The newcomers probably already used the light, maneuverable war chariot which was to make their name a terror throughout Asia Minor, and they spoke the Indo-European Hittite language.

Where they came from can only be guessed at. Apparently they were just one more group of those mysterious "Aryans." But we do know a lot of other things about them.

The Hittites were a fierce and warlike people, more interested in forging their formidable iron weapons and training their horses for the next battle than in tame agricultural pursuits. Even their undeniable architectural talents were best displayed in the superb military fortifications which guarded their cities.

In appearance they were not an attractive people. They were stockily built, with heavy features and large, hooked noses. "Parrot faced" is an unflattering but accurate term applied to them by Sir Harold Nicholson. Nowhere do we find the appealing grace of the Egyptians or the Cretans.

Nor was their mode of dress calculated to help much. Judging from the surviving statues and reliefs, fashion decreed that men wear high, conical hats and long boots resembling those of a mountaineer except for their queerly turned-up toes. For the rest, some are dressed in long, heavy robes, but most wear only a short, wraparound kilt, tightly belted in at the waist. Women appear less often, but the goddesses at Yazilikaya are attired in cylindrical head-dresses and long skirts that appear to be pleated from the waist.

Hittite art must be judged mainly from reliefs similar to those of Yazilikaya, from pottery, and from small seals. Examples of sculpture in the round are few and not overly successful, although there are a few delightful figurines. One of the most charming of these is now in the possession of the British Museum. It represents a sturdy little man skillfully fashioned in gold and typically attired in conical hat, short tunic, and turned-up boots. His large-featured face wears a rather disdainful expression, and he strides along with folded arms in the cockiest manner imaginable. Possibly this is intended to be the portrait of a real man, but it is more likely that the haughty little creature was a god, for Hittite art devoted itself mainly to religious subjects.

In this connection, it came as something of a surprise to

These carved Hittite reliefs located in remote mountainous areas, remained undiscovered for 3,000 years.

discover that the deities represented in the reliefs at
Yazilikaya were not Hittite but Hurrian in origin. Perhaps
the shrine was inspired by Queen Pudahepa, Hurrian wife
of Hattusilis III. The Tudhaliyas of the inner shrine was
certainly her son.

Whatever the reason, there seem to have been few home-
grown gods or goddèsses in the Hittite pantheon, and the
most important were always Hurrian. Possibly because
Anatolia is subject to severe and terrifying storms, the
greatest of these was Teshub, the Weather God. Hebat was
sometimes designated as his wife, and the pair had a son,
Sharruma or Sharma, the Young God.

Scores of other deities were adopted from all over
Mesopotamia, and each is clearly portrayed with his or her
identifying symbol in the reliefs. One would almost believe
the ancients had problems in keeping them all straight too.
Perhaps the strangest is the so-called Dagger God. He is
shown with a human head, a body composed of four crouch-
ing lions, and, instead of legs, a broad tapering blade
disappearing into the rock.

The purely literary content of the Boghazköy archives
was mainly concerned with myths and legends about the
numerous beings whom they worshiped. There is some
poetry, and many of the state documents are couched in
narrative form. The rest covers many phases of life in the
Hittite Empire.

Kingship among the Hittites may have once been an
elective office filled probably by the ablest military commander. We find them ruling in early times with the advice
of a group of nobles which was called *pankus,* though this

practice died out later. Gradually the king became more powerful until we find one who refers to himself as "my Sunship." Ultimately, it came to be believed that a king did not die — he simply "became a god."

A king's duties were manifold, for he served not only as supreme commander in the field but as religious leader and chief judge. All this was in addition to his normal duties as head of state. Religion seems to have taken precedence, however, for we read of a king turning over his military command to a subordinate only when he had to hurry home to preside over some festival or rite. Generally, he was a warrior-king in the summer, a priest-king in the winter.

Hittite queens were a powerful and independent lot, retaining their position even after their husbands' deaths. As long as the queen-mother lived, her daughter-in-law could not bear the title of queen; she was referred to merely as "the king's wife." Later, she would get her chance to be powerful, too. Pudahepa, wife of Hattusilis III, was associated with her husband on all state documents and possessed her own official seal.

Members of the royal family filled the most important state offices. Together with nobles, fighting men, and servants of the crown, they formed the ruling classes and probably served as the advisory board, or *pankus,* to the monarch.

The great bulk of the population, the Hattians, possessed no power at all except possibly in local affairs. They were mostly peasants, but there were craftsmen— "men of the tool" — including potters, builders, weavers, leather workers and smiths. Such men were free but subject to forced labor for the state.

There were slaves as well, but their position is puzzling. A master apparently had the power of life and death over them, but he was not held responsible for their crimes. A slave might own property or even marry a free woman, and the law code sets compensation for his injury at exactly one half that of a free man.

The economy was primarily an agrarian one. Oxen, horses, mules, and asses served as draft animals; sheep, goats, pigs, and cattle furnished food and wool. Vines, apple, pear, pomegranate, and olive trees are mentioned in the tablets, as are barley and emmer wheat, which was used for both bread and beer.

Copper, silver, lead, and iron were mined from the surrounding mountains both for local manufacture and for trade. Silver in bars or rings was the medium of exchange; the shekel and the mina were the monetary units.

Warfare seems to have been the only occupation of the higher nobility, and they had developed a formidable fighting machine in which the terrifying charge of chariots played an important role. Hittite kings seem to have been master tacticians, capable of forcing battle on open ground where their chariotry would be most effective. Generally, they relied on the element of surprise, but when siege proved necessary, they could bring up effective siege machines.

To administer all this there had to be laws. Two nearly complete tablets, each listing one hundred clauses, make up what some scholars believe to be the entire basic law code. Compared to Hammurabi's savage eye-for-an-eye, tooth-for-a-tooth justice, Hittite laws are surprisingly mild. Most offenses, including murder, were punishable only by a fine, and law recognized degrees of responsibility just as we do today — that is, killing by accident drew a lesser punishment than murder with malice.

The listed rules cover a variety of legal matters from marriage and "accidents at a river crossing" to sorcery and offenses connected with vineyards and orchards. They also list fixed rates of pay for various services and set the prices for certain foodstuffs, for clothing, for livestock, and for land. For the sum of three shekels, for instance, one might purchase either three live sheep, one acre of irrigated land, the skin of a full-grown ox, the meat of thirty calves, or a fine shirt.

Little is known, however, of the actual application of these codes, and they seem to modern jurists to be woefully inadequate, since they deal only with special cases or unusual circumstances.

By far the greatest value of the Boghazköy archives lies in the wealth of historical details revealed there. From the royal decrees, diplomatic correspondence, and treaty negotiations recorded, the shadowy Hittite Empire emerges in vivid colors to take its place in history.

The first firm historical reference to the Hatti is in the annals of King Sargon of Akkad somewhere around 2300 B.C. A Hittite poem dating from 1400 B.C. tells how seventeen kings, among them Pamba, King of Hatti, banded together to fight Sargon's grandson, Naram-Sin, about 2200 B.C. This story is of dubious value, however, for another version of Naram-Sin's war exists on a Babylonian tablet, and different names are listed.

The letters of Assyrian merchants living in Kanesh about 1900 B.C. tell of two Kings, Pitkhanas and Annitas, who were probably Hattite father and son. Annitas is known from another source in which he tells of his many conquests. Among them was the city Hattusas. Not satisfied with destroying that city, he placed a terrible curse on anyone who should dare to rebuild it. The relationship of Annitas with the next recorded ruler is not known, for a gap in the records lasts until 1740 B.C.

The Tudhaliyas who ascended the throne of Hatti then was a Hittite, and succeeding kings proudly traced their ancestry back to him. But little is known of him or of his son, Pusharruma.

True Hittite history begins with King Labarnas, for he was a mighty warrior and conquered much territory. Of him a later king wrote, "He destroyed the lands and made them powerless, and he made the seas his frontiers. And . . . his sons went each to every part of the land . . . and the great cities of the land were assigned to them." The lands are listed, and it would seem that this early king ruled over as great an area as could be claimed by much later and more powerful monarchs.

It was Labarnas II who defied the ancient curse and rebuilt the city of Hattusas as his capital. To commemorate his daring, he then changed his name to Hattusilis, builder of Hattusas. He was succeeded by a grandson, Mursilis, who proved to be a vigorous and successful king. Among his more notable feats of arms was a daring, if rather senseless, attack on Babylon.

"Against Samsu-ditana, the men of Hatti marched, against the land of Akkad," and not even mighty Babylon could withstand the ferocious onslaught of the Hittite chariots. King Samsu-ditana was killed and the city put to the torch. The fall of the Queen of Cities was noted in the records of every civilized land, making this one of the firmest dates in ancient history.

Mursilis did not live long to enjoy his triumph. He was slain by a brother-in-law, Hantilis, soon after his return to Hattusas, and his violent death ushered in a long period of anarchy and confusion. King after king was assassinated in that bloody game so popular in ancient court circles — the palace revolution. Meanwhile, Hantilis and his successors managed to lose most of the territory conquered by Labarnas, Hattusilis, and Mursilis. Not until 1525 B.C. did a monarch arise who was strong enough to put a stop to the chaos.

Telipinus, although another usurper, was a remarkable man. It was he who wrote a constitution for his country which set forth precise rules to govern the succession. He also advanced for the first time in history the idea that a king was neither absolute nor divine, and he delegated to the *pankus* the power to pass judgment on the king's action. They could even execute him if he were found guilty of bad government — or the murder of one of his relatives! So now we know how Telipinus hoped to escape the assassin's knife.

Telipinus never gained back all the territory that had been lost, but he made great strides. He is also the first king to negotiate a treaty with a foreign power. We know that it was with the Great King of Kizzuwatna, but we do not know its terms.

In the forty years which followed the death of Telipinus, four kings sat on the throne he had made secure, but the first of any consequence was Tudhaliyas II. He founded a new dynasty at a time when it looked as if the Hittite empire might go under. Enemies on every side, encouraged by the growing power of the Hurrians and Mittanians, who grew bold enough to attack and take Hattusas herself, closed in on every side. "The Hatti lands were sacked from beyond their borders," and the empire barely survived through several weak reigns.

In 1380 B.C., Suppiluliumas seized the reins of the faltering empire in strong and capable hands. But before he set out to regain lost territory, he tried to consolidate his power at home. It was he who fortified his mountain stronghold with the great walls discovered by Texier. Excavation has shown them to be masterpieces of defensive architecture and well worth a closer look.

The natural defences of the site at Boghazköy needed little reinforcement except on the south, where an open plain invited attack. It was there that the mighty walls arose which are still standing after thirty-three centuries. The line of defense was double — a high wall with a lower, secondary one thrown out about 20 feet in front.

The main work consisted of inner and outer shells connected at intervals by cross walls. The hollow rectangles

thus formed were filled with rubble. The outer shell was
built of massive stones, carefully cressed into rectangular
blocks which fit snugly together without mortar. Both walls
were fortified every 100 feet with projecting towers which
allowed the defenders to set up a murderous cross fire
against attackers. Both ran along the top of a high, stone-
faced rampart.

The three main gateways were flanked with blocks of
masonry which extended the entire width between the
double lines, so that all who entered must pass under sur-
veillance of the towers. Finally, a tunnel led from inside
the city completely under walls and rampart and out onto
the plain. Presumably, this was to allow the defenders to
make a surprise sortie without opening the main gates.

Suppiluliumas must have felt he was leaving his city
secure when he set out to punish the upstart Mittanians
for their recent depredations. Unfortunately, his armies
were thrown back by those same upstarts. Nothing daunted,
the Hittite king simply marched his troops through the wild
and hostile mountain regions to the north and attacked
Mittani again, this time from the rear.

The surprise was highly successful. Mittani fell, and the
way was open for reconquest of the lost Syrian territories.
Hittite chariots soon overwhelmed the king of Kadesh and
penetrated as far as Damascus before they stopped. The
reconquest was complete a few years later when Carchemish
surrendered after only eight days of siege.

Suppiluliumas was king when the boy Tutankhamen
ascended the throne of Egypt, and he sent rich gifts in
congratulation. Among them were awls, chisels, and a

dagger with a hilt of gold and diamonds, all made of iron.
How strange it seems that so common a metal should ever
have been considered a fitting gift for a king. Yet, in those
days, it was rarer and more precious than gold, and far
more useful. And, though objects made of meteoric iron
were not unknown, the Hittites alone possessed the secret
of extracting the metal from ore. Some sources say that the
process was invented by a barbarian tribe called Kiwadana
who were subject to the Hittites, but, whoever invented it,
it became a jealously guarded monopoly of the kings of
Hattusas.

Before Suppiluliumas died of plague in 1340 B.C., he
had made himself master of Asia Minor and Syria from the
borders of Egypt to Assyria. He was succeeded by a son,
Mursilis II, who proved as able as his mighty father and
even enlarged the empire. He crushed the powerful kingdom
of Arzawa to the west, conquered Azzi-Hayasa to the east,
marched ten times to quell disturbances among the wild
border tribes to the north, and pacified a revolt in Syria
to the south. Between campaigns he even found the time to
write poetry, some of which has been preserved.

Mursilis died in 1306 B.C., leaving a consolidated empire
to his son, Muwatallis. The new king immediately embarked on a war against Egypt, which he was to wage for
nearly a quarter of a century. The high point of this conflict
came at the almost legendary battle of Kadesh in 1286 B.C.

The honors of the battle went to Hittite arms, for
Muwatallis scored a resounding victory over Rameses II.
The wily Pharaoh, however, succeeded in extricating his
army from the trap which would have destroyed it, a feat

which he had recorded upon the walls of Thebes as a smashing victory.

Muwatallis' son, Urhi-Teshub, was put aside by an uncle, Hattusilis III. "Out of respect for my brother, "wrote the new king, 'I loyally did not act selfishly, and for seven years I complied. But then that man sought to destroy me . . . and . . . I complied no more but revolted from him." We do not know Urhi-Teshub's side of the story, but it is doubtful that he could have successfully rebutted the usurper's closing argument. "If he had never quarreled with me, would the gods have made him, a great king, lose to a petty king?"

Hattusilis rebuilt Hattusas, which had been sacked during his brother's reign, and recopied the archives. It was also he who gave one of his daughters as a wife to Rameses II, to seal the peace treaty of 1269. Perhaps they were prompted by mutual fear of the rising power of Assyria, but the ancient enemies now formed an alliance which would last for seventy years. Even the queens of the two lands exchanged letters of congratulation for the occasion.

Hattusilis was the last of the great kings of Hatti. Under his successors the once-great empire steadily deteriorated. Like wolves at the kill, enemies attacked from all sides to tear great chunks of territory from their weakening grasp. Still, there was enough left to fight over and a Hittite king was on the throne when the last great wave of invaders came in from the west.

Known only as the "Sea People," these new enemies proved irresistible. It was in 1190 B.C. that they came, and, according to an Egyptian scribe, "The isles were restless,

and no land stood before them, beginning with Great
Hatti."

Indeed, Great Hatti virtually disappeared from the face
of the earth. Her cities toppled — the mighty fortress hidden
in the mountain fastnesses of Anatolia was deserted, and
its very name was erased from the memory of man. Never
again would the earth tremble beneath the terrifying
charge of Hittite chariots.

In the southeastern provinces of Syria, the traditions of
Hittite civilization were remembered dimly for another five
hunded years, though their origins were forgotten. Then
this so-called neo-Hittite state became a thorn in the side
of Assyria, and late in the seventh century it was destroyed.

All that remained then were the strange and challenging
inscriptions and the forlorn and crumbling walls, which in
time would lead scholars back through the centuries again
— to bring to light once more the ancient splendors of the
silent cities of Great Hatti.

5 Great City Shang

Back in the 1890's in China, two old friends sat talking of their mutual interest in the ancient writing of their ancient land. One was ill, and at one point he interrupted the conversation to prepare a dose of medicine. The doctor's prescription specified that he grind up a certain amount of "dragon bone," enough to cover the point of a knife, mix it with tea and drink it.

It sounds like a very strange prescription to us, but such bones have been regarded as powerful medicine for many centuries by the people of China, and they were an important part of every druggist's stock. The bones themselves were much older than the custom, however. They were, in fact, quite often the fossilized remains of extinct prehistoric animals, as excited paleontologists had already discovered.

To the two friends both the prescription and the bones were quite commonplace. But as the sick man carefully prepared the prescribed dosage, mixing it in a turtle shell, his friend noticed something very strange about this particular shell. The light seemed to catch on a series of scratches on its surface which looked very much like writing. Closer investigation proved them to be just that, an ancient form of the Chinese script.

Mr. Wang I-jung and Mr. Liu O had made a very important discovery!

Together they searched the stocks of bones in the drugstores and found more specimens of inscribed bones and shells. Despite the natural reluctance of the druggists to reveal their sources of supply, it was soon determined that most of them could be traced to a single place — Anyang, a site on a bend of the Huan River in northeast China. The farmers of the village of Hsiao-t'un Ts'un dug the relics out of their fields and sold them for a few coppers (pennies).

Mr. Wang and Mr. Liu bought every bone they could find which bore a legible inscription and set to work to translate them. They were only partially successful, but what they did discover was exciting enough. Mr. Wang died during the Boxer Rebellion of 1900, but Mr. Liu continued the work. He made careful rubbings of over one thousand of the very best specimens, and these he published in a six-volume work entitled: *Turtle Shells from the Iron Cloud Studio.* The inscriptions in this collection dated from 1765 to 1123 B.C.

Mr. Liu fell into political disgrace and was banished, and his fabulous collection of "dragon bones" was allowed to scatter. But other scholars had taken up the quest. For the inscribed bones and turtle shells were not just ancient doodles. They were the recorded questions and answers of a type of fortune-telling popular in many ancient societies. It was called scapulimancy.

Furthermore, these were not just ordinary questions. These were the oracle bones of the shadowy, all-but-unknown Shang Dynasty, and they recorded intimate details from the reigns of at least ten Shang Kings.

Still, the site at Anyang went uninvestigated. Some scholars remained skeptical. The high prices commanded by the dragon bones with writing on them encouraged a booming business in forgeries, and frauds were frequently unmasked, casting doubts on the authenticity of all such relics. Besides, the Chinese reverence for the dead made it difficult to obtain permission to disturb the long-buried civilization.

Meanwhile, irreparable damage was being done by bone hunters. Not to be outfoxed, the farmers of the area had also banded together and started their own excavations. They were forced to give it up after a small but bloody war broke out over property rights.

But at last in 1928 Dr. Tung Tso-Pin, a Chinese scholar, persuaded the *Academia Sinica* to let him explore Anyang. The first scientific digs proved disappointing. Although for as long as anyone could remember, bones and shells had been exposed by every rain and spring plowing, this year very little turned up. Trench after trench was barren of important finds. Enthusiasm reached a low ebb.

Then on October 23rd, trench number 36 was begun on the property of a Mr. Lu. It would very likely be the last to be dug, for the fierce fall storms already piled their threatening clouds on the horizon.

To everyone's amazement, trench 36 proved a bonanza of good-sized oracle bones and turtle shells. The men worked feverishly, and when the fall storms broke, four days later, putting an end to the season's digging, the trench was already 2½ feet wide by 22 feet long by 15 feet deep. By then, there seemed to be little doubt that Anyang had been an important center of the Shang civilization.

Until that time very little was known of China's history prior to the ninth century B.C. Only myths and legends carried farther back than that, and myths and legends told of a Great City Shang which lay somewhere on the banks of the Huan River. But there had been nothing to show that such a city had ever really existed.

In 1929 Carl Bishop of the Smithsonian Institution and Dr. Li Chi joined forces to continue the Anyang excavations. Once more the results were disappointing. Trench 36 seemed worked out, and new ones yielded little. In one mound north of town they did find a sectioned mold for the casting of bronze but somehow failed to grasp the true import of the discovery. Only when someone was inspired to dig under the beaten earth of the village threshing floor were the dreams of spectacular finds realized. There, among scattered potsherds and oracle bones, was the body of a boy, apparently drowned in a flood which swept through the center of the city. Nearby graves yielded valuable specimens of pottery and bronze.

Though Dr. Li was convinced that here at last was the Great City Shang of the legends, nothing could be found of the expected palaces and temples beyond some pounded-earth foundations. Unlike other civilizations farther west, the Chinese did not use stone or brick for building houses, and their structures did not survive well. Then, too, the stratigraphy presented many problems. The yellow earth had been churned for untold centuries by floods, well diggers, and bone seekers. Mixed in among the Shang relics were evidences of occupation levels stretching from a Neolithic people all the way to the modern.

Only after many seasons of digging has the picture become clearer. Today, many of the questions can be answered with reasonable certainty, though wars and political unrest have made the study of the site very difficult for western scholars.

Who, then, were the Shang? What were they like? How did they live? Where did they come from?

The people of this advanced Bronze Age culture seem to have appeared with dramatic suddenness on the plains of northeastern China in the eighteenth century B.C. Physically they were quite similar to their modern descendants. Portrait masks show the typical oriental features quite clearly. Though scholars admit that many aspects of their culture could have developed in China, and there is no real evidence to point to any other origin, most of them believe that the Shang civilization was patterned, however remotely, on the achievements of the great societies to the west.

From their first appearance they possessed many of the basic attributes of an advanced culture, including a fully developed and complex writing system with thousands of characters. Most of the forms of modern written Chinese were known and used by the Shang, from whom it is a direct inheritance.

Historic details of these people are scarce. Legend tells of a bold warrior-king named P'an-keng, (1401-1374 B.C.) who swept down upon the Neolithic people of the plains and brought nearly two thousand of their villages beneath his heel to found the Shang Empire. Arrow and lance tips of stone, bone, and bronze have been found lying thickly around the earthen walls of some of the excavated villages, offering mute testimony to the power of the invaders.

P'an-keng ruled his new territories from a city he founded on the banks of the Yellow River some distance south of the Anyang site. It was left to his successors to move north to the bend of the Huan and found their capital of Great City Shang. The new site was well chosen and the city grew and prospered. The later kings of the dynasty all ruled from there. Oddly enough, although the earlier site, Cheng Chou, was heavily fortified, no trace of walls has been found so far at Anyang.

Together, the years of excavation and the evidence of the oracle bones afford us a fairly clear picture of life in the Shang capital. The city itself was composed of rammed-earth foundations with wooden columns supporting roofs of mud-coated bamboo or thatch. No trace of the tiles used so widely in later times has ever been found. Walls, even at this early date, may have been only light weight screens of wood or lattice.

The design of these buildings seems to have been quite similar to those of recent times. Houses usually boasted only a single story with gabled roofs. Some were modest, roughly 10 by 15 feet, but others have revealed dimensions as impressive as 30 by 150 feet.

The largest may have been the palaces of the Shang Emperors. Here among the courtyards and temples they

The Great City Shang revealing great art in bronze and marble.
Marble works shown here.

reigned in splendor and magnificence that must have seemed almost supernatural to the rude, barbaric peoples whom they had conquered. To those who had never known anything beyond a few thatched dugouts huddled within mud walled compounds, the great city which now arose in their midst must have been awe-inspiring.

By modern standards, of course, it would have seemed small and overcrowded and even squalid. The narrow, unpaved streets teemed with merchants and artists, musicians and courtiers, priests and slaves; all the motley multitudes that go to make up any city. Here, bronze-helmeted soldiers strode along, spears clanking to the rhythm of the march. There a nobleman drove his glittering chariot on the way to court, or a high-born lady was borne along in her gilded palanquin.

Perhaps she was on her way to the shop of her favorite jeweler. The evidence suggests that here, as in many eastern cities today, there were close-knit groups of artists and artisans, each occupying its own section. Potters, sculptors, workers in bronze, carvers of stone, shell and bone, weavers, basketmakers — all plied their trades here, bartering their goods for the cowrie shells which were the medium of exchange.

The Shang bronzes, with their intricate designs and lovely blue-green patina, are justly regarded as among the most beautiful objects ever made by man. They are considered priceless, but an occasional piece may change hands for as much as ten thousand dollars. These precious relics have been found in many different sizes and shapes. Some are as much as three feet high, and though they were originally cast in intricately carved molds, no two have ever been discovered exactly alike.

It would be a mistake to believe that the consummate artistry of the Shang was restricted to their work in bronze. Though no actual examples have survived, impressions have been left in the earth of woven materials so delicate they could have been fashioned only from the finest of silk. Tiny little buttons were elegantly carved for use with these gossamer fabrics. Other buttons of marble and shell and bone have come to light, as have the painstakingly carved shell combs and hairpins which adorned the long hair of both sexes.

Examples of the sculptor's art range from small jade figurines to semi-human monsters cut from white marble. Black marble and limestone were also common. The prevalence of such objects is surprising, for Chinese artists have seldom worked in this medium.

Jewelers were skillful and much in demand. They produced elaborate designs in bone and shell as well as jade, turquoise and ivory. Even the Shang horses wore harnesses heavily decorated with bronze and sometimes inlaid with semi-precious stones.

Chime stones, drums and an instrument called a *hsüan* are not uncommon, implying not only skilled instrument makers, but a well developed taste for music. Musical accompaniment seems to have played an important part in religious rites and military campaigns as well as for sheer entertainment.

Such luxuries as we have been describing were available, of course, only to the rich and noble. Little is known of the lower classes, and few of their dwellings or possessions have survived. There may, indeed, have been only one lower class aside from slaves — the peasants who produced food for the city dwellers.

Were they primarily herdsmen or farmers? We know that they had domesticated most of the animals we raise today. Twenty species have been identified from the Anyang site, including dogs, horses, sheep, goats, oxen, water buffalo and pigs. Some evidence even suggests that chickens may have been raised, but this is uncertain. Even elephants were known, but not being native to China, they were probably imported to aid in the work of heavy construction.

Nevertheless, animal husbandry appears to have been fairly unimportant to the Shang economy. Although the oracle bones occasionally record skirmishes with invaders over grazing lands, there is not much evidence that the herds were considered a major food source. They seem to have been reared primarily to furnish victims for the sacrificial rites of the priests. In this context it must be remembered that these people considered sacrifice as the actual feeding of the spirits.

Agriculture was vital. Prayers for rain or fair weather in season bulk large among the oracle bone inscriptions. The king and his ancestor gods were held in some measure responsible for the vagaries of the weather, and the success or failure of a reign was measured by the accuracy of its weather forecasts.

Not much is known of the crops upon which they lavished so much care and prayer. Millet seems to have been the basic cereal. Wheat is mentioned and so is rice, but the complex irrigation system upon which widespread rice cultivation would have depended is not in evidence. A plant which yielded a coarse fiber similar to hemp completes the inventory of known crops. It is certain that there must have been many more, but beyond these the records are silent.

Much more is known of the life of the upper classes. Politically speaking, Shang was a city-state ruled by hereditary kings called *wang*. They appear to have been absolute monarchs, though they were served, and possibly advised, by twenty or more titled officials.

Of these the *yin* were the most important. Their duties were many and varied, ranging from responsibility for agricultural programs to managing the affairs of the royal household. The *tso-ts'e* were the record keepers who wrote down the important happenings of court and empire. There were even men called *kung* whose sole duty it was to provide the king with musical entertainment.

Also attached to the court were the *shih,* priests who offered the sacrifices to the gods. Most important of all, however, was a special class of priestly diviners called *shen-jen*. Theirs was the task of interpreting the will of the gods as it was imparted to the people by means of the oracle bones.

As is often the case among a warrior nobility, hunting was the favorite sport, and it was often practiced on a grand scale. A royal hunting party would travel great distances and slay animals by the hundreds. Dogs and beaters were used to drive deer, wild boar, badgers and rabbits within range of the huntsman's spear or the mighty bow of the archer. Sometimes specimens were captured alive for the royal zoo. One day's catch is recorded as consisting of "one tiger, forty deer, 164 foxes . . . " and a host of smaller animals.

In war the Shang were formidable opponents. Much of their military success was due to the use of chariots, which the flat plains of northern China allowed them to maneuver with almost parade ground ease. A Shang king could thus concentrate his picked shock troops at any threatened point with astonishing speed. The chariots were drawn by two, sometimes four, horses, and while they seem to have been used primarily to transport the warriors to the scene of battle, it is possible that the Shang had mastered the technique of charging them in massed ranks like cavalry. It is interesting to note that the modern Chinese character for "wheel" or "vehicle" is simply a picture of one of these chariots seen from above.

One type of bronze armor has survived, and it is believed that others, made of leather and reinforced with bone or wood, once existed. Bronze helmets were often decorated with fierce animal faces and topped with a hollow socket to hold an ornamental plume.

Shang warriors were armed with bronze-tipped spears, battle axes and the wickedly pointed, double edged dagger-axe called the *ko*. There was also a light-weight bow which was probably used for hunting and target practice as well.

Possibly the most amazing weapon in the Shang arsenal, however, was a bow of laminated wood, bone, and sinew. It was so powerful that it required a pull that has been

estimated at 170 pounds and that was capable of shooting
a spearlike arrow over protecting walls at a range of a
quarter of a mile or better. It is difficult to see how a people
as small in stature as the Shang could ever have wielded
so heavy a bow — unless, as has been suggested the archer
lay on his back and flexed the bow with his feet.

It seems unlikely that a Shang king maintained more than
a small standing army. One thousand to fifteen hundred
men would have been quite sufficient for his predatory raids
against the primitive villages, which went on constantly.
Nevertheless, he could and did raise armies estimated as
high as thirty thousand strong when circumstances demanded it.

Such an army must have been an impressive spectacle
as it marched out to meet the foe — the sun glinting
brightly from the polished surfaces of bronze armor and
chariots and lance tips, innumerable plumes tossing from
helmet tops, battle flags snapping in the breeze. How martial
the roll of the great war drums must have sounded as they
set the cadence for the marching feet.

Of course, no war or any other major project was undertaken without the blessing of the oracle bones. It is directly
due to the Shang passion for knowing the will of the gods
on the most trivial matters that we owe much of our knowledge of their civilization. Their religion included a form of
ancestor worship which still plays an important part in the
lives of the Chinese peasants. Those who had departed
this world were revered for their wisdom and experience
which could be of immeasurable value to the living. They
were also very touchy and must be treated with all possible

respect, lest they become offended and visit dire punish-
ments on the irreverent.

There were other gods, including an all-powerful being
named *Ti*, and numerous lesser deities and demons who
must be consulted and propitiated. This was most often
accomplished by means of the oracle bones.

The question to be answered or the request to be granted
was carefully inscribed on a piece of polished bone or the
lower shell of a type of now-extinct tortoise. Many kinds of
bone were used, including at least one human skull, but the
tortoise shell seemed to be used most often for the petitions
of royalty. One estimate puts the number of such bones
excavated in northern China in excess of 100,000!

After the bones were carefully scraped and polished,
several oval-shaped depressions were drilled in their surface.
To receive the answer of the gods, the *shen-jen* now heated
the prepared bone, possibly by placing a hot coal in one
of the depressions. The heat caused expansion, and
eventually cracks appeared. The cracks were usually two in
number, roughly across the axis of the drilled oval and at
right angles to each other, forming a crude T. It is interesting to note that symbol like a T lying on its side still means
"fortune-telling" in modern Chinese script.

Careful examination and interpretation of the cracks by
the priests yielded the answers of the gods.

This method of fortune-telling and prophecy did not by
any means originate with the Shang. Their only contribution
to an otherwise ancient art was the inscription of the
question directly on the bone or shell. Caches of such bones
have been discovered so neatly arranged that one cannot

escape the conclusion that they were methodically filed away by the priests and kept for future reference, perhaps to check the accuracy of their predictions.

The gods, though kept busy with such vital concerns as weather forecasts and weighty decisions on matters of state, were equally willing to answer such purely personal questions as those concerning the recovery of a sick person or the sex of an expected child. It seems to have been the custom for the king to consult the oracle at least once in every ten days — the Shang week — and he always carried his tortoise shell with him when he traveled, just in case.

As might be expected, the practice of ancestor worship called for something rather elaborate in the way of burial customs. Many of the wonderful works of art were created solely to ornament the tombs of the dead kings and nobles of Shang. Unfortunately for archaeology, the very wealth of such burials insured that, almost without exception, the tombs would be looted of their finest treasures. Indeed, a set of bold bandits once filched several valuable bronzes from a grave almost under the noses of a scientific expedition, which was digging just across the river.

Enough remains, however, to allow archaeologists to reconstruct the pomp and circumstance which attended a royal burial. Digging the grave was no mean project in itself. One measures 60 feet square at the top and descends with steeply sloping sides to a depth of 43 feet. The main entrance faced south, where a ramp 150 feet long descended gradually to the tomb's floor. There were shorter, steeper ramps on the other three sides.

Within the large pit smaller ones were often dug. As

many as nine have been found in a single tomb, each containing the skeletal remains of a dog and an armed man. Presumably they had been killed and placed there to guard the treasure of their dead master.

Next came a chamber of heavy hewn planks, the inner side plastered, painted, and decorated with inlays of boar's tusks. Earth was tamped between the outer side and the walls of the excavation. The shelf thus formed provided space to set out the grave goods. Every conceivable luxury — bronze vases, statues, fine fabrics, jades, food, and weapons — were crammed into the available space.

The coffin lay in the center of the walled area, and more treasures were heaped around it.

But it was not only the material comforts which were to accompany the dead monarch to the next world. He must have companionship and recreation too. To this end his horses and dogs were often led into the pit and slain. Once it was the entire royal zoo.

All too often a royal burial demanded human victims as well, sometimes in great numbers. These unfortunates, perhaps prisoners of war, were herded down the sloping ramps and beheaded almost on top of the coffin. For some reason not altogether clear, the severed heads were sometimes buried in a separate part of the tomb.

Not until everything possible had been provided to keep the honored dead happy and content in his grave was the pit filled in and smoothed over. Now it was no longer necessary for the king to consult the oracle bones to know the will of the gods. It was rather up to his successor on the throne to seek advice and favors from *him*, for he had now become an ancestor god himself.

But despite the protection of all the gods, tragedy came at last to the Shang Empire. After nearly six centuries of unchallenged military supremacy, the mighty armies finally met their match. Down from the western highlands swept a wave of fierce warriors, fifty thousand strong, to crumple their defenses and shatter their forces in the field.

It was the old story of a highly developed civilization falling before the relentless surge of a more barbarous one. The invaders were called the Chou, and their leader, Wou Wang, was known as The Martial King. Steadily he drove the defenders back until the capital city itself was in his grasp.

When it became apparent that nothing would stop the advance of the Chou, the last of the Shang kings arrayed himself in his most costly robes and adorned himself with his most fabulous jewels — but not in honor of his conqueror. Rather than accept the bitter consequences of defeat, the proud monarch threw himself into the flames of his blazing palace.

So died the Shang dynasty but not the Shang culture. Much of that was adopted and absorbed by the conquerors and, in turn, by their conquerors, until many of the arts, religious beliefs, and customs of modern China can be traced back in unbroken succession to the silent city beside the Huan River.

6 The Mysterious Tyrrhenians

Almost any excavation in certain parts of the Italian Peninsula can prove both exciting and profitable. Every spadeful of earth turned — whether by a well digger, a construction crew, or even an amateur gardener —holds the possibility of uncovering some relic of the past. And nowhere have such finds been more frequent than in the area enclosed by the Arno and Tiber Rivers, backed by the mountain spine of the Apennines and fronted by the sea.

This territory, which today includes Tuscany and parts of Umbria and Lazio (Latium), is one of the most varied and beautiful parts of Italy. More important, it was once the homeland of the mysterious civilization we know as Etruscan.

Dionysius of Halicarnassus recorded at least three traditions to account for the presence of the Etruscans here. 1.) They were Pelasgian invaders from Thessaliotis who changed their name after conquering the natives. 2.) They were Lydians from Asia Minor who did the same. 3.) The Pelasgians came first but were later ousted by the Lydians. The second of these theories is that recorded by Herodotus, and he makes a very dramatic tale of it.

In the days of Atys, the son of Manes [13th century
B.C.], there was a great scarcity through the whole land
of Lydia. For some time the Lydians bore it patiently,
but finding it did not pass away, they set to work to
devise remedies for the evil. . . . The plan adopted
against the famine was to engage in games one day so
entirely as to feel no craving for food and the next
day to eat and abstain from games. In this way they
passed eighteen years. Still the affliction continued
and even became more grievous. So the king divided
the nation in half and by drawing lots determined
which portion would stay and which would leave the
land. . . . The lot was cast, and the losers . . . sailed
away in search of new homes and better sustenance.
After sailing past many countries, they came to Umbria
in the north of Italy, where they built cities for themselves. . . . They laid aside their former name of
Lydians and called themselves Tyrrenians, after the
name of the king's son, Tyrrhenus, who led the colony.

Classical literature offers several corroborations of this
story. Thucydides confirms Herodotus' statement that the
Tyrrhenians once settled on the island of Lemnos, presumably on their journey of migration. A gravestone discovered
there in 1885 bears two long inscriptions in an alphabet
and language strongly resembling those of Etruria. Several
potsherds inscribed in much the same manner have been
discovered there since, lending color and credence to the
Asian migration theory.

But Dionysius refused to accept it: "Because the
Etruscans have in common with the Lydians neither

language nor laws, nor do they worship the same gods. Therefore, those who say that the Tyrrhenians are . . . natives . . . seem to be nearest the truth, for they are a very ancient people and unlike any other in language and customs." So now we have a fourth theory: The Etruscans were not invaders at all; they had been there all the time.

Prehistorians of today are convinced, however, that the earliest Iron Age settlers, a people they call Villanovan, actually did come by sea from the eastern Mediterranean between 1000 and 900 B.C. Beyond that nothing is clear. Whether they were Pelasgians or Lydians, whether there was one invasion or two still remain in question.

Whatever their origins, the Etruscans were a wealthy and powerful people who first began their climb to greatness some three thousand years ago. They dominated northern Italy from about 750 B.C., and their sphere of influence ranged from the Alps to Sicily, from Marseilles to the Adriatic.

Unlike the Hittites, they were never lost, never forgotten. Scholars and historians, from the Greek poet Hesiod, who made them descendants of the gods, to the Roman Emperor Claudius, who devoted twenty volumes to them, were intrigued by the enigma of the Etruscans. Unfortunately, most of their material has been lost to us, and only a few tantalizing fragments remain. The ancient cities of Etruria are hidden under the walls and houses of modern towns, and their cemeteries, like those of Egypt, have been so heavily plundered that much of their information-yielding value has been lost.

Lovely works of art in terra-cotta and bronze we have in

plenty, along with weapons of antique design, domestic equipment of superb workmanship, and many examples of elaborate jewelry in gold and precious stones. Such things have been ardently sought after by collectors of "antiquties" for centuries, and every museum in Europe boasts extensive collections. Most of them are virtually useless to science, however, since the precise location in which the articles were found cannot now be determined.

Interest in the Etruscans began to stir at the time of the Renaissance, when Europeans first started reexamining the classical past. Early in the seventeenth century, Thomas Dempster, a Scottish scholar living in Italy, wrote the first full account of these mysterious people. His book, *Royal Etruria,* was not published until a century after his death, and when it did come out, in 1723, it caused a sensation. Suddenly scholars everywhere were excited over these long-dead people and their culture.

Within five years, excavations of a crude sort were under way at Volterra, site of ancient Velathri. In 1739, a tomb was discovered there containing forty burial urns. In 1738 at Palestrina, ancient Praeneste, a bronze coffer was unearthed. It was cylindrical in shape, with engraved panels presenting the mythical story of the Argonauts and their voyage in search of the Golden Fleece. It is believed to date from 330 B.C.

Such finds as these only encouraged the greedy tomb robbers to intensify their search. In the years that followed, hundreds of graves were plundered for the sake of the antiquities which found a ready, if illicit, market. The magnificent tomb furniture was scattered, and the priceless murals were left to decay, their value to archaeology destroyed forever.

The first systematic digs were not begun until the early part of the nineteenth century, under the patronage of Prince Frederick of Prussia. There was certainly no lack of sites to excavate. In 1828, a farmer peacefully plowing his field saw one of his oxen suddenly sink into the ground — its weight had broken through the thin crust covering an underground vault, which turned out to be an Etruscan tomb. Within a year after the incident, over two thousand specimens of beautifully wrought vases of bronze had been recovered from the area.

That same year, 1828, the first scholarly work on the mysterious people of ancient Tuscany was published — *The Etruscans,* by Karl Otfried Müller, German classical philologist. Twenty years later, the British consul, George Dennis, wrote a book called *Cities and Cemeteries of Etruria,* a kind of guide book to modern Tuscany, describing out-of-the-way places and ways of life. Scholars found it most useful in their investigations into parts of Italy which had not, until then, been closely explored by archaeologists.

Since that time, the excavations have gone on almost without interruption, and our knowledge of the mysterious Etruscans has been widely expanded.

Before 1000 B.C. there was nothing in northern Italy to justify the name of civilization. The people who inhabited those fertile plains and valleys had advanced little beyond the New Stone Age, and their knowledge of bronze was still in the rudimentary stages of development.

Then, quite suddenly, everything changed. The slow

developments of the Bronze Age were skipped over, and an
Iron Age culture was in full bloom in Tuscany. The break
was so dramatic and complete that it is almost impossible
to account for it except by invasion.

The Bronze Age people had buried their dead; the
Villanovans cremated theirs and deposited the ashes in
funerary urns, the covers of which were sometimes in the
shape of helmets. Many urns of Latuim are shaped like
miniature houses, complete with steeply thatched roofs,
smoke holes, and decorated ridgepoles. The early people
had been semi-nomadic herdsmen; the newcomers brought
with them new methods of farming which allowed them to
build permanent settlements on easily defensible sites.

They also introduced many articles of Greek and Near
Eastern origin which are found in their tombs. The souls
of the departed, here as elsewhere, were furnished with all
those things considered necessary for life beyond the grave.
The men had their weapons and tools of iron and bronze;
the women their needles and mirrors and jewels and those
most indispensable of all feminine possessions, their bronze
fibulae or safety pins.

By the middle of the eighth century B.C., however,
another drastic change had taken place. Cremation was no
longer fashionable. The dead were now interred in stone-
lined tombs under heaped-up mounds of earth called
tumuli. These tombs grew ever more elaborate and ever
richer in grave goods. Metal and pottery vases and votive
figures showed far more imaginative designs. The Villanovan
zigzags and beading gave way before such Near Eastern
motifs as palms and rosettes and winged lions and to scenes

from the Greek myths. Writing, which now made its appearance for the first time, was done in an archaic form of the Greek alphabet, but it recorded, not Greek, but a non-Indo-European language.

While there were Greek influences, the culture as a whole had something of a Near Eastern flavor. The religion was a highly ritualistic one which laid great stress on foreseeing the future by examination of the entrails of sacrificial animals. A bronze model of a sheep liver discovered near Piacenza in 1877 bears a striking resemblance to those of

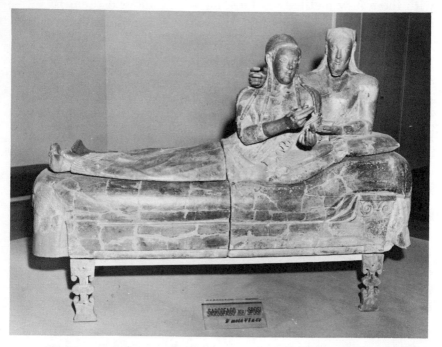

Etruscan statuary, sixth century B.C. — sarcophagus of newlyweds.

Babylon. It also bears the name of some thirty Etruscan gods, most of them unknown.

Social customs were very different, too. The women, for instance, were influential and respected members of Etruscan communities and were accorded honors and allowed a degree of freedom unheard-of by their less fortunate Greek sisters.

The language puzzle is what most frustrates scholars. Multitudes of inscriptions mock at us from engraved bronzes, carved stones, and painted walls. But they remain largely untranslated. Scholars have no difficulty *reading* the familiar Greek script — the trouble is that rarely can they understand the words it spells.

The Roman writer Livy, speaking of his ancestors, states, "I have it on good authority that in those days young Romans learned Etruscan letters as they now do Greek." What a precious find just one Roman schoolboy's copybook would be for the linguists! Or Claudius Caesar's Etruscan grammar! So far as we know now, the language Roman youths studied has no relationship with any other. It remains, for us at least, unknown and seemingly unknowable.

Part of the difficulty of translation lies in the shortness of the inscriptions. Of the ten thousand or so known, only a few consist of more than a single line, and many of them are not proper sentences but simply names or dates.

Oddly enough, one of the longest texts was not found in Etruria at all, but in faraway Egypt. It was written on a long roll of linen which somehow found its way across the sea to be used as wrapping for a mummy. How such a thing happened is one of those intriguing mysteries which will probably never be solved. It does, however, give us over 500 different words out of a total of 1,135. Though it is recognized that the text concerns religious matters, it cannot be translated.

Scraps of glossaries compiled in ancient times, a few short bilingual texts, and a lot of shrewd guesswork have furnished us about one hundred identifiable words. We know that *capy,* for instance, meant "falcon"; *aisar,* "gods"; *etera,* "slave"; *phersu,* "actor"; *cassis,* "helmet"; and *lautni,* "freedman." Those that can be guessed from their repetition on tomb inscriptions include the words for "year," *avil;* "day," *tin;* and family relationships such as "mother," *ati;* "wife," *puia;* "son," *clan;* "daughter," *sech;* "grandson," *nefts.*

Possibly the most tantalizing find consisted of only six words — *mach, zal, thu, huth, ci* and *sa.* These words were inscribed on dice, one on each face of the cube, and almost certainly correspond to the numbers "one" through "six." But which is which? Even the tempting assumption that they follow the modern relationships of "one" opposite "six" and so forth is not capable of proof.

A few recognizable proper names complete the tiny list of known words. The rest must wait for a fortunate discovery — perhaps that dream of all linguists, a long bilingual text. Unfortunately, it seems unlikely that even this would give us all the answers, since two thirds of the inscriptions are religious, and little survives which might conceivably be classed as literature.

Meanwhile, scholars pursue other avenues in their search

for information about the ancient Etruscans. There is
much to be learned from the writings of the Greeks and
Romans. From such sources we have gained an insight into
customs and the history of these mysterious people. Under
the careful scrutiny of the archaeologists, their cities and
cemeteries have revealed much more.

Etruria, like Greece, was divided into a number of
independent city states. Unlike the bickering Greeks, however, Etruscan cities seem to have maintained strong ties
with one another. Twelve original cities formed the loosely
organized Etruscan League. Each was ruled at first by a
priest-king called a *lucumon,* though these lucumons were
later replaced by magistrates elected for a period of one
year.

As the civilization spread, new groups of twelve cities
were founded in the Po valley and on the plains of
Campania. Each new area had twelve, for twelve was a
sacred number. At the height of Etruscan power, their cities
and colonies were spread the length and breadth of Italy,
on the islands of Sicily, Elba, and Corsica, and even in
North Africa. At least forty-seven sites are known.

Many of these are occupied today by modern cities. Pisa,
Arezzo, Orvieto, Perugia, Siena — the list is a long one —
can boast examples of Etruscan handiwork in foundations,
walls, and gateways. Even mighty Rome was once ruled
by Etruscans. Other sites were deserted long ago. Some
survive only as names; others, like Tarquinii and Veii, have
left identifiable ruins which yield important archaeological
evidence. It is doubtful, however, that any Etruscan city
has yet been thoroughly excavated.

The first population centers of Etruria were located near, but not on, the coast of the sea which bears their name, the Tyrrhenian. The land they controlled was rich in natural resources. There were fine stands of timber; the forests swarmed with game; and fields and pastures were volcanic and amazingly fertile. But the real basis of Etruscan wealth lay in the extensive and easily worked mineral deposits which veined the hills. The seemingly inexhaustible supplies of iron, zinc, copper, and tin they mined found a ready market with their less fortunate neighbors, either as raw material or as manufactured goods.

In return, the Etruscans acquired gold and ivory and gem stones and all the myriad things that went to make life pleasant or to adorn their tombs after death. To facilitate the exchange, Etruscan trade routes stretched far beyond the towering mountains to the north and criss-crossed the seas in all directions.

Their merchant navy found snug retreat in the many fine natural harbors with which their coastline was blessed. And if we are to believe the Greek chroniclers of the time, its captains did not confine themselves to such profits as might be picked up in honest trade. Raids against Greek and Carthaginian colonies were so frequent — and so successful — that Strabo seems to be overcome with wonder at the fact that the citizens of Caere were *not* pirates.

It is hardly suprising to find that Greek writers are not too enthusiastic about such rivals, for the wealth of Athens was dependent upon commerce too. At least once, however, the two were allies. Thucydides tells us that during the famous naval battle at Syracuse in 413 B.C., three 50-oared Etruscan galleys fought on the side of the Athenians.

The very fact that they were considered a threat by such powerful enemies as Athens and Carthage indicates the extent of Etruscan naval power.

The chief victims of these piratical forays were southern Italy, Sicily, Corsica, and Sardinia, but occasional raids were also launched against the coasts of France and Spain. It was considered particularly outrageous that they carried off statues and an occasional young priestess from the temples. One Greek legend has them kidnapping Dionysus, but he, being a god, easily made his escape after turning his captors into dolphins.

Somewhere around 540 B.C. the Etruscans allied themselves with Carthage and succeeded in driving the Greek settlers out of Corsica. This was the high point of their sea power and a rather hollow victory for Etruria. Carthage went on to take Spain and North Africa and gain control of the Straits of Gibraltar. Greece still held Sicily and her southern Italian colonies.

Caught now between the two strongest navies in the world, Etruria's control of the seas slipped from her grasp.

On land she was more successful for a while. Except for Umbria and the Greek colonies far to the south, virtually the entire peninsula was under her dominion. Historically speaking, by far the most important conquest was that of the dirty, unimpressive little village which nestled in the hills, guarding an easy crossing of the Tiber. The village was called Rome, and the year of its conquest was 610 B.C.

The Etruscan rulers of Rome were the Tarquin kings of later history, hated by the Romans. The first of them is credited with the building of the Circus Maximus and the introduction of horse and chariot racing, wrestling and boxing, as well as building walls, draining marshes, and the construction of the Forum Romanum and the Temple of Jupiter. His successors carried out his plans and contributed much of their own to the glory of Rome.

Legend has it that they were driven out in a revolt led by Lucius Junius Brutus, and in 509 B.C. the small village by the Tiber, now grown to a thriving city, began its remarkable career as the Republic of Rome.

The loss marked the beginning of the end for Etruria. All attempts to retake Rome were heroically repulsed, and the southern colonies, cut off from their mother cities, fell before the growing power of the republic. Soon that power was great enough to reach northward and attack the Etruscan League on its home ground.

Between 437 and 406 B.C. there was almost constant warfare between Rome and Veii. Then the determined Romans sat down to a ten-year siege before finally taking the city by storm. Livy tells us that "the day was spent in the killing of Rome's enemies and the sacking of a wealthy city." The people of Veii were enslaved, its gods were carried off to Rome, and the city leveled to the ground.

If the members of the Etruscan League had doubted the power of Rome before this, they were now shaken out of their lethargy, but it was too late. Marauding Celts were pouring across the Alps to attack them from the north. The same year — some ancients say the same day— that Veii fell, the Celts took Melpum, an Etruscan city whose site is today unknown. It may have been some comfort to the Etruscans to know that Rome suffered from these incursions too. She was sacked in 381, but she was soon wealthy enough to buy immunity.

The Etruscan cities were not so fortunate. Every city in the Po Valley fell, and the cities of Tuscany were open to the fierce raiders. About 310 B.C. those still free allied themselves with the Umbrians, and all other enemies of Rome including the Gauls, but to no avail. Legend has it that the impregnable city of Cosa was visited by such a plague of mice that the rodents accomplished what the Romans could not, and the city had to be abandoned.

The others fell to more conventional foes until, in 282, only Vulci and Volsinii remained free of the Roman yoke, and even they were doomed. Vulci went first, Volsinii held out desperately until a slave revolt within her beleaguered walls ended her resistance. Now every Etruscan city was subject to Rome.

So complete was their defeat that even when Hannibal marched his army across the Alps in 217 B.C., fully expecting to find allies among the conquered cities, the Etruscans dared not break the Roman alliance, though they must have been sorely tempted.

Certainly, when, in the Roman civil wars of the first century B.C., some of them chose unwisely to side with Marius against Sulla, they sounded the final death knell of Etruria. The triumphant Sulla savagely laid waste to their cities, deprived the citizens of their rights, and confiscated their wealth.

One last flicker of Etruscan independence came in 41 B.C. when Perugia was foolish enough to offer asylum to Lucius Antonius, brother of Marcus Antonius (Mark Anthony) and by then a sworn enemy of Octavian. For her pains the city was starved into submission and burned to the ground. Seutonius quotes a story that the furious Octavian chose three hundred prisoners of knightly or senatorial rank, and offered them on the Ides of March at the altar of the deified Julius Caesar.

The Etruscan civilization, as such, vanished from the face of the earth. Her language was no longer heard; her achievements were forgotten.

But she was mighty even in death!

Aside from her ruined cities and her magnificent tombs, she left other less perishable legacies, some of which survive to this day. Her greatest memorial was deeply ingrained in the very structure of the civilization which destroyed her.

For the Romans, while professing an undying hatred and scorn for their ancient enemies, adopted much of the dying culture as their own. Practically no facet of that civilization which we recognize today as peculiarly Roman is without its influence from the people they detested.

Though one ancient writer scornfully refers to Etruria as the creator and mother of superstition, Roman state religion reflected their belief in divination and interpretation by *harispices,* whose methods, like their pointed head-dresses and curving staffs, were purely Etruscan.

The famed military organization of the Roman legion

was patterned after the Etruscan triple formation of light, medium, and heavy infantry. Military triumphs for war heroes were also a feature of the Etruscan scene. So was the sound of military trumpets.

In civil affairs we find that crowns and rings and scepters were all symbols of Etruscan authority. So were the *fasces* — bundles of sticks bound around the handle of an axe and carried before an official on formal occasions. This symbol can still be seen on our Mercury dimes. The toga of the Roman patrician was borrowed from Etruria and the so-called imperial purple was the color worn by Etruscan royalty.

In the first flush of enthusiasm over these discoveries, there was a strong tendency for scholars to assume that everything worthwhile in Rome was a legacy from Etruria. This is not necessarily the case. While it is true that Etruscans were constructing superior roads and canals and aqueducts while Rome was still a primitive settlement, there is now some question that they ever really understood the principle of the arch as a structural rather than a decorative element. And, though the Romans themselves referred to their houses with balconied rooms around an open court as "Tuscan," there is little archaeological evidence to support the assumption that the design originated there.

The list of Roman "borrowings," of which only a few have been mentioned, is long enough to show that the city on the Tiber owed much to its one-time masters. In exchange, the Roman writers have given us fascinating, if highly critical, glimpses into the lives of those masters. The picture which emerges is that of a complex and very human society.

On one hand we see an essentially gay and pleasure-loving people, who filled their homes with luxuries and their days with feasting and drinking. The men were addicted to the pleasure of the hunt; the ladies loved to adorn themselves with elegant robes and fabulous jewels. Both men and women seem to have indulged in dicing and gambling.

Dancing girls or troupes of boy and girl dancers were in much demand as entertainers, and there seems to have been a great fondness for music. Roman historians credited them with invention of the military trumpet, and the fact that they had at least six types of trumpet seems to bear this out. Pipes or flutes, however, were even more popular, and several varieties were in use. The lyre was also a favorite, but the singing which usually accompanied this instrument seems to have been unknown.

In contrast to such carefree pastimes, we find much apprehension about the future and an urgent need to know the will of the gods at any given moment. Religion in Etruria was bound up in their efforts to learn such things through omens and auguries. Lightning, thunder, the flight of birds, the entrails of sacrificed animals could all be interpreted in accordance with the sacred books to foretell coming events.

The gods who controlled their destinies were many and varied. Some can be easily identified with their Greek or Roman counterparts by their names. *Uni* was Juno; *Maris,* Mars; *Aritimi,* Artemis; and *Aplu,* Apollo. Others bore

Etruscan names but can be equated to familiar dieties, among them *Tinia,* Zeus, and *Turan,* Venus. One of the strangest names is *Fufluns* who seems to have been the Etruscan Dionysus. A third group of purely Etruscan gods have no counterpart in any other religion, and their duties and attributes are obscure. *Muantrns, Culsans,* and *Klanins* belong here.

The most striking thing about Etruscan religious beliefs, however, is their preoccupation with death. Here, too, we find inexplicable contrasts. Their love of the good things of life is reflected in the elaborate tombs, which indicate that they rather expected the next world to be only a continuation of earthly joys. But there is also a note of gloom, especially in the later periods, when scenes of demons and ghosts, and dismal journeys to the underworld begin to appear more often. Dark-winged deities with snake-infested hair hover menacingly to snatch away the souls of the unwary.

On the whole, though, the tombs indicate an attitude of cheerful anticipation of the pleasures to come. We see the deceased, modeled life-size in terra-cotta, reclining on his couch-shaped sarcophagus as though he were merely resting for a few moments before the feast. We see him again on the painted walls, joyfully throwing himself into the sport of the chase or quietly listening to music or watching the gyrations of a dance. Time and again the murals reveal scenes of festive gaiety in which men and women eat together, drink, laugh, and love as they did in life.

Nor are their surroundings any less luxurious than those they knew before. The tombs, carved out of the soft, volcanic rock, were often large and richly embellished suites of rooms, designed to serve as family burial vaults for generations. They were exquisitely furnished with all the comforts and treasures which so delighted the pleasure-loving Etrurians.

Especially beautiful are the many examples of the metal-worker's art. Goblets of gold and silver worked with scenes from other lands; weapons and armor of bronze inlaid with precious metals; little bronze statues, some quite modern-istic in style; even elaborately decorated bronze chariots have been recovered from the tombs of Etruria.

And the jewelry! Marvelous earrings and pendants and headbands of such delicate and exacting workmanship that it amazes today's experts. Styles range from massive repoussé work to airy filigree lace. Some pieces are made entirely from tiny gold beads arranged in intricate patterns.

No wonder Etruria has long been an archaeologist's paradise! Modern science has some wonders of its own to contribute to the study of Etruria. Aerial photographs of Tuscany show a landscape dotted with whitish patches which are not apparent from the ground. Each marks the location of a grave mound which long ago disappeared, and hundreds of new sites have been discovered by this method in Tarquinia alone. Enlargements of the photo-graphs can even provide exact details of size and shape. Electronic detection devices have been used successfully to discover the hollows within the earth which betray the presence of a burial chamber.

Then, too, a special camera can be lowered through a small shaft drilled into one of the chambers and rotated

to photograph every nook and cranny. Thus, the archaeologist can determine whether or not the tomb is likely to
repay the time and money spent in excavating. Photographs
taken by this method were once relayed to New York
immediately, and thousands of people on this side of the
Atlantic were treated to the sight of a tomb no *living*
human being had laid eyes on for thousands of years.

Each new tomb which is opened affords fresh and exciting glimpses of the distant time when the gay and
mysterious Tyrsenoi ruled Italy from the now-silent cities
of Etruria.

7 Who Built Zimbabwe?

Solomon, the much written about king of the Hebrews, ruled from the city of Jerusalem during the tenth century 974-937 B.C. Biblical sources tell us that during his reign he embarked on ambitious building programs and maintained a fabulously lavish court. But where did the ruler of such a notoriously poor land acquire such riches?

It was no secret. The wealth of Solomon, says the Bible, came from the mighty fleets which he had built at Eziongeber, a port on the Gulf of Aqaba, which leads to the Red Sea. These ships, manned by Phoenician sailors furnished by King Hiram of Tyre, set sail at stated intervals. Three years later they returned, heavily laden.

The cargo? It was a fantastic mixture — ivory and incense, apes and peacocks, gold and silver and precious stones, all the exotic treasures so dear to the hearts of the ancients. One report sets the value of a single shipment of gold at the staggering sum of 420 talents. A single talent would be valued today at $32,640!

And it all came from a fabulous land called Ophir!

Ancient Ezion-geber is known. The Red Sea has receded over the centuries, leaving the one-time port high and dry, but an American expedition in 1938 brought it to light from under the drifting sands. Among other things, they discovered the great smelting furnaces used to reduce tons of metal. And today Israelis are bringing the ancient region back to life.

But where was the land of Ophir?

Many scholars believe that Ophir was only another name for the land of Punt, described in Egyptian temple paintings. It was to this mysterious land that the female Pharaoh, Hatshepsut, once sent her ships to bring back cargoes of gold and myrrh in fantastic abundance. The voyage took more than a year to complete.

But not everyone agrees with this theory. Nearly every remote coast in the world has been a candidate for the site of the fabled land of gold. It has been known by many names — Ophir, the Land of Punt, Prester John's Kingdom, the Earthly Paradise of Adam and Eve. Columbus had even dreamed of finding it when he set forth to seek the Indies. The Solomon Islands in the South Pacific were so named, because their Spanish discoverer thought he had found the fabulous source of King Solomon's wealth.

But gradually the field was narrowed to the east coast of Africa, specifically the Sofala coast of Southern Rhodesia. Ibn Battuta, Moslem globetrotter of the fourteenth century, stated that the Sofala interior was called Yoûfi. "From Yoûfi," he wrote, "they bring gold dust to Sofala." And Yoûfi sounds very much like Ophir to those eager to find a resemblance.

Small wonder then that the first Portuguese adventurers lent willing ears to the tales they heard of a great stone city far inland along the Zambezi River. A man named De Goes was the first to describe the city, though it is considered most unlikely that he ever saw it, even from a distance. He reported a "fortress built of large and heavy stones inside and out." Another Portuguese, De Barros, treasurer of the newly formed colonies, says emphatically, "It is not possible that these buildings could have been built by the blacks."

He, too, is believed to have based his observations on hearsay. Both men seemed to have favored the Devil as the architect, just as the Spanish were to credit that worthy gentleman with the massive buildings of Mexico and Peru.

As far as we know, the first white man actually to see the fabled city was an American hunter, Adam Renders, who accidentally stumbled across its ruins in 1868, centuries after the first reports. For Renders the tumbled, overgrown ruins held little interest, and he left them undisturbed after only a cursory inspection. It was not until the German geologist, Karl Mauch, explored the site more thoroughly in 1871 and pronounced the ruined buildings the work of a "civilized people of antiquity" that the world began to take notice.

Mauch expressed the opinion that the two most important structures were the palace of the Queen of Sheba and a copy of Solomon's temple at Jerusalem, built, of course, by Phoenician architects. It was an opinion to stir the imagination. By the time that a force of British soldiers camped near the ruins in 1890, this theory was so firmly established that one of them wrote lyrically, "The Englishman is in the land of Ophir!"

More importantly, if Ophir was indeed found, then King Solomon's mines could not be far away. Soon the silent reaches of the Zambezi and Limpopo Rivers became the focal point of a wild gold rush. Though none was really very near the mysterious, stone-walled city, many ancient gold mining works were found and, unfortunately, destroyed by the treasure seekers. By the year 1900 fourteen thousand gold claims had been registered in the area. It will never be known just how many of those fourteen thousand miners were smashing priceless archaeological evidence in working their claims.

Nor did the city itself go unscathed in the mad hunt for gold. It was ransacked as early as 1888, when an explorer named Willi Posselt found some interesting soapstone birds but little gold. In 1895 William G. Neal, a prospector, formed "The Ancient Ruins Company, Limited," selling stock to raise the necessary cash for exploring the ruins. But his expectations of his discoveries were overoptimistic, and he was out of business by 1900. In 1902 the first ordinance was passed to protect the ruins from such exploitation at the hands of unscrupulous men, but tremendous damage had already been done.

Neal had thoroughly explored only forty-three of the 140 ruins known to him personally (over five hundred are known today), but he reportedly recovered only five hundred ounces of worked gold. How much treasure was melted down and never reported? Only by comparison with the one or two unplundered sites discovered since that time can we even make a guess; but it must have been a lot.

By now the whole world had heard of the "Phoenician" cities of the African jungle and wanted to know more. In 1905 the first responsible explorations were undertaken by David Randall-MacIver on behalf of the British Association. Randall-MacIver's findings were not at all welcomed by those who espoused the Phoenician theory, which had been so ably defended by Richard N. Hall in his seemingly well-reasoned and scholarly publications.

For, in all the seven sites he examined, Randall-MacIver unearthed not a single object dating from earlier than the fourteenth century A.D. What is more, the buildings were not Egyptian, not Phoenician, not even Arabian. They had all been designed, constructed, and occupied by native Africans!

This was quite an unexpected blow to those who were convinced that the ruined buildings must have been built by foreigners and in the ninth century B.C. There must be some mistake! Surely Randall-MacIver was suffering from a touch of the African sun to believe that ignorant savages were capable of constructing these projects! Everyone knew that the thatched hut was the limit of their architectural ability!

Despite the fact that two powerful civilizations were known to have existed in Africa in ancient times, modern man has persisted in regarding the entire continent as "dark" and uncivilized. Both black and brown natives — according to popular beliefs — have always been savage, childlike, backward. How, then, could the sophisticated Zimbabwe culture have arisen, unless it was imported from a more "civilized" land?

Though only the most ignorant could possibly believe such a thing today, it must be remembered that many startling discoveries have been made in Africa only during this century. It is one of man's newest revelations that his history stretches back farther on the continent of Africa than anywhere else in the world.

There are rock paintings in Northern Rhodesia that date from 4000 B.C. Dr. and Mrs. L. S. B. Leakey excavated a Neolithic site in Kenya in 1937 which had been lived in for three thousand years before it was abandoned about the time of Christ. More important to our argument, evidence of an Iron Age culture exists in Northwest Rhodesia in the first century B.C., and there was a flourishing one at the south end of Lake Tanganyika at least fifteen hundred years ago.

Perhaps it was to settle the heated arguments arising from Randall-MacIver's report that the British Association sent out a second expedition in 1929. It was headed by Dr. Gertrude Caton-Thompson, and the eminent archaeologist's findings were in complete agreement with Randall-MacIver's. According to her reports, the disputed buildings were certainly no earlier than the fourteenth century, perhaps even as late as 1750. All objects premedieval in date were of *African* origin, and there was absolutely no trace of Oriental or European influence in the architecture. As a final blow, radiocarbon dating placed the very beginnings of occupation at the Zimbabwe site somewhere around A.D. 500.

In the face of such overwhelming evidence that, not only
the ruined city of Zimbabwe, but every similar site in
Southern Rhodesia was of African origin, it was time to
take a closer look at the early records, which had all too
often been ignored by the theorists. Once preconceived
notions were discarded, the evidence of a flourishing Negro
civilization was not too hard to find.

In 1517 Duarte Barbosa, a Portuguese adventurer, had
written of a great kingdom called Benametapa lying somewhere inland from the coast of Mozambique. Traders,
Barbosa reported, made a twenty-six day journey to the
large town of *Zimbaoche* to barter their tawdry cloth and
glass beads for a fortune in gold. Zimbabwe lies about
250 miles inland from the ancient port of Sofala, and it
would not be impossible to travel the distance in the time
alloted by Barbosa for the traders' journey.

The ruins are some 17 miles east of modern-day Fort
Victoria and only a few miles off the main highway from
Salisbury to Johannesburg. One need no longer trek through
the jungle to view the tall walls, the gateways, the towers,
and the strange monoliths which have caused so much
speculation and argument. The entire valley is studded
with ruins which lie half hidden among low patches of
dusty green shrubbery. They are built of the granite which
weathers in convenient layers from the surrounding hill-
sides — great, roughly rectangular slabs of stone which often
weigh many tons.

Two important complexes dominate the scene and
command the attention of the visitor. One, the so-called
Acropolis, frowns down forbiddingly from the summit of a

Zimbabwe Ruins.

steep-sided hill. It seems to have been intended as a
defensive work, for it is surrounded by a partially destroyed
ring wall over 12 feet thick and can be approached only by
winding, easily defended passageways.

A cave which opens into the ninety foot precipice below
the Acropolis walls is said to have such weird acoustics that
a normal male voice can be heard in the other major
structure, the Elliptical Building, six hundred yards away,
but nowhere else in the valley. It does not take much
imagination to realize that the priests of Zimbabwe must
have found effective uses for such an unusual quirk of
nature!

This second group of buildings is surrounded by walls
which sprawl in a 220 by 300 foot ellipse across the plain
below. The walls still stand an impressive 30 feet in height
and are 20 feet thick at the base. They are slightly curved
and slant inward toward the top — both well-known tech-
niques for adding structural strength. They are not con-
tinuous, however and were deliberately built with puzzling
gaps which would have made them useless for defense. It
has been assumed that these gaps were once filled with the
outer walls of long-vanished buildings of some perishable
material.

Drains were provided at the base to prevent rainwater
from backing up within the enclosure, and the walls were
topped with stones laid in a decorative zigzag or chevron
pattern. This pattern, incidentally, looks a little like some
primitive inscription and may account for the "carved
inscription, so old that no one knows how to read it" that
was mentioned by De Goes.

Inside the walls, evidences of smelting and metalworking activities have been found, lending some color to the legends of gold. Smaller walls run hither and yon among steep flights of curved steps, timber-linteled doorways, closed passages, tall platforms and strange, conical towers. The largest of these stood 35 feet high before Mauch tore off the top courses of masonry in his treasure hunt. No wonder he and Hall were so certain that they had found the fabled land of Ophir!

"The King of Benematapa," wrote De Goes, "keeps great state, and is served on bended knees with reverence." And now there is little doubt that he kept that state at Zimbabwe, nor that Zimbabwe flourished as the political, commercial and probably religious center of a Negro empire which encompassed thousands of square miles.

But it was not always so. According to Dr. Caton-Thompson, the site had been occupied almost continuously since about the second century A.D. It first residents were people of a Stone Age culture, possibly Hottentot, who lasted for approximately two centuries. Crude stone axes were about their only legacy. Then the stone workers were driven out or subjugated by an ironworking people who came in from the north. Oddly enough, neither here nor at any of the other sites is there any evidence of a Broze Age culture. Arrowheads, ax and hoe blades, and spear tips, all made of iron, beads and other small ornaments, and broken pottery give their evidence of the second occupation. Not one of the objects is more than seventeen hundred years old.

The ironworkers flourished and their culture reached its

climax from the eighth to the tenth centuries but had gone
into a decline before they fell before a new invasion. The
newcomers, whose ruler was titled the *monomatapa,* held
sway from the twelfth to the fifteenth century, at which time
new invaders occupied the site. These people, various Shona
tribes, seem to have held Zimbabwe until the eighteenth
century.

The great stone walls were probably raised about 1600.
The people who built them were the organizers of the far-
flung empire that De Goes and others wrote about. They
left us their copper and gold wire, mostly in the form of
coiled ankle bracelets; soapstone bowls, some bound with
fine gold wire, some carved with geometric or pictorial
patterns; rings; necklaces; iron swords; bone tubes; pottery
jugs and many items of foreign manufacture which they
had received in trade.

Molds for the casting of iron ingots have been found in
two peculiar forms. One is shaped roughly like a cross, the
other like a letter H. Ingots in both these forms were used
as currency and have been found as far away as Ireland —
though, of course, there is no proof that they came from
Zimbabwe.

Theirs was a purely Negro culture, though the people
were probably of Bantu stock and brown of skin rather than
black. Unfortunately almost all skeletal remains have
perished in the unfavorable climate. Only eight specimens
were found by Dr. Caton-Thompson, none of them dating
back more than eleven hundred years. Scanty as they are,
they bear out the other evidence. All were of the Negro
race, again probably Bantu.

It is believed that the rulers were not of the same race, though no one knows who they were. There exists the fascinating possibility of ancient links with Ethiopia in their history, but this must remain another unsolved mystery for the present. In their own mythology, the first king was the moon who took as his wives the morning and evening stars.

The later rulers retained something of the mythical character. The strange conical towers of Zimbabwe are one of its most unusual architectural features. Tall and hollow, they rose from a circular base with sides that sloped inward to a much smaller diameter at the top. They apparently were built to contain the umbilical cords and jawbones of deceased monarchs. The kings were worshiped as gods after death, if not before, and the towers were their shrines.

A living king was surrounded by much pomp and ceremony. When His Majesty walked abroad, he was preceded by heralds beating drums, and he carried carved rods as symbols of his authority. Some of these ceremonial drums contained the bones of a human hand, and their ghostly rattling added a touch of the supernatural to the royal procession.

The monamatapa, or king, was always richly robed in garments of silk, obtainable by trade with Sofala. And, since drums and women seem to have been the symbols of royalty, it is only to be expected that the King of Benametapa should be well supplied with both. One source tells of a monamatapa who kept a harem of three thousand, seven or eight of whom were chosen as his principal wives. Many of these were his sisters. Indeed, the true queen, or *mazarira,* whose children were the heirs to the throne, had to be one of his sisters — a custom reminiscent of ancient Egypt.

Quite unexpectedly we find that the royal harem wielded a certain amount of power. Should a king be ceremonially killed, as he sometimes was, to fulfill the requirements of certain religious rituals, the women of his household were responsible for the choice of a successor.

On the other hand, their fate could be quite horrible. A dead king was buried carefully, though not embalmed. All possible honors were paid him, and his grave was furnished with every available luxury and comfort. His wives were sometimes required to accompany him, and they were either killed outright or shut up in the sepulcher to live out the short time left them with the decaying body of their lord.

It is harder to guess the purpose of the queer, rough-hewn monoliths. Standing about thirteen feet high and tapering to a crude point, they were probably of religious origin. As such, they have their counterparts in many scattered areas of the world. The carved soapstone birds were probably cult items, too, and so peculiar to the site that, until quite recently, one of them adorned the flag of Southern Rhodesia.

The religion to which they belonged seems to have been only the primitive worship of inanimate objects and animals plus a cult of the dead. Two great religious festivals were celebrated yearly, one in May, the other in September. Mock battles and human sacrifices seem to have played major parts in these rituals. There were also mass pilgrim-

ages to the acropolis or to the temple to make spiritual contact with the dead kings, whose oracular messages still
guided their people from beyond the grave. The eagle and
the lion were both superstitiously regarded as reincarnations
of these ghostly rulers and were therefore considered sacred.

Certain church documents claim conversion to Catholi-
cism of one of the *monomotapas* early in the seventeenth
century. If so, it made no lasting impression except in a
treaty which granted "gold mines" to Portugal in 1629.

Somewhere around 1700, the flourishing Zimbabwe culture fell before an invasion by the Rowi, another tribe of
Shona stock. Under a leader called the *mambo* they took
over the city, but their occupation was short-lived. In their
turn they gave way to the Nguni from somewhere to the
south, and eventually, the site was abandoned to the
ravages of nature.

The silent city was never looted by the blacks, who
continued to live in the land it had once ruled. Even today
they regard the ruined walls with superstitious awe. Only
with great difficulty can any native be persuaded to set
foot within its precincts.

Some, though by no means all, of the gaps in the story
of the Zimbabwe culture have been filled in from other sites.
A different but especially interesting story is told by the
sacred city of Mapungubwe, some 200 miles away.

For many years tantalizing rumors had filtered through
to the white settlers of a sacred hill where vast treasures
were supposed to lie hidden. Somewhere in the wilderness,
they whispered insistently, was a fabulous city of gold, but
no one could ever pin the rumors down. At last, a farmer-

prospector named Van Graan determined to find the legendary city and reap its golden harvest for himself. In 1932, accompanied by his son and two other men, he set out.

It was no easy task they had undertaken. The natives who knew of the city considered it "a place of fear," and could not be persuaded even to point in its direction. So deep-rooted was their fear that they were careful to turn their faces in some other direction when the city was discussed among them. To climb those forbidden heights, they warned, meant certain death. Its treasures were dedicated to the great ones among their departed ancestors and must not be disturbed. Not one soul, it seemed, was brave enough or foolish enough to defy the wrath of its long-dead inhabitants.

Nevertheless, Van Graan persisted, and his patience was finally rewarded. He found one man, more enlightened than his neighbors, who agreed to point the way for the little party. That way led into the northern Transvaal just south of the Limpopo, that great gray, green, greasy river made famous in Kipling's *Just-So Stories.*

There, rising almost vertically from a scrub-covered valley, was a small table mountain, 100 feet high and 1000 feet long. On top of the mountain, the guide informed them, was the city they sought.

He also showed them how to scale those forbidding cliffs. Eagerly now, the treasure hunters cut their way through a tangle of thorn and scrub to find the narrow, carefully hidden rock chimney where a vanished race had once cut slots for their ladder rungs. A difficult climb brought the panting men to the top of the precipice. On its very brink they encountered a breastwork of loosely piled stones still standing menacingly where they had been placed long ago, ready to be toppled down on invaders foolhardly enough to storm the sacred city.

Beyond this wall lay a plateau littered with the debris which is the ugly and universal aftermath of human occupancy. Broken pottery, bits of metal, beads, discarded stone weapons lay about everywhere, but Van Graan and his party had no time to waste on such common things. A recent downpour had gouged deeply into the loose topsoil, and here and there the bright African sunlight winked back the yellow glitter of newly exposed objects of gold!

For once, it seemed, the legends had spoken truly. Feverishly, the men began to search in earnest. Beads, bangles, and broken flakes of the precious metal gleamed in every handful of earth. Large plates were found, some in the shape of rhinoceroses. These had once been fastened to carved wooden forms with tiny golden tacks. One gold-bedecked skeleton was found and carefully dug out, but without the proper preservatives the fragile bones crumbled to dust upon exposure to air.

Within a very short time the little party had gathered 75 ounces of pure gold. After some discussion, it was decided that they should keep it all for themselves and say nothing to anyone of their discovery. Fortunately for the cause of science, the younger Van Graan was not happy with this decision.

The boy knew something of the exciting finds that were being made in Africa, and he was well aware that this new discovery had a far greater value than mere gold. To ease his troubled conscience, he confided the whole story to his former teacher, a man of some learning named Fouché. The older man lost no time in submitting samples of the gold to the Royal Mint, which reported them to be of great purity and the first examples of wrought gold ever discovered in the area.

Thanks to the boy and his teacher, the Union Government was able to acquire an important, unspoiled site, and the University of Pretoria was entrusted with its excavation. Almost at once a very strange feature came to light. Van Riet Lowe reported that the summit of the sacred hill was covered with thousands of tons of soil which had apparently been transported from the surrounding countryside. And every ounce of it had had to be carried up those precipitous walls by human labor — a stupendous task!

In 1934 a "royal" burying ground was discovered which contained parts of twenty-three skeletons. Each had been buried with numerous objects of gold and other metals. One grave contained no less than 70 ounces of purest gold. In another, the leg bones were entwined with over one hundred bangles of coiled wire. All told, they yielded a fortune in gold plated objects and over 12,000 gold beads!

The finds at Mapungubwe are important for two reasons: the skeletal remains which are all too rare in South Africa and the fact that it was virtually unplundered. Like the famous tomb of Tutankhamen in Egypt, Mapungubwe serves as a tantalizing example of the glories of a vanished culture. Yet it adds very little to our knowledge of the medieval African people as a whole.

Here was another Iron Age people whose kings lived in isolated magnificence and were buried with enormous wealth. But exactly what their connection with Zimbabwe was is still uncertain. They built no monumental buildings as did their northern neighbors, although stone platforms for their huts are present on the sacred plateau. They seem to have flourished at the same time, for radiocarbon dating of the skeletons gives an age of at least one thousand years. Still there is no evidence of direct contact between Zimbabwe and Mapungubwe.

There are even a few additional riddles.

Why did the people of Mapungubwe choose to live on that lonely hilltop? Were they conquerors, ruling a subjected tribe from their inaccessible stronghold? Or were they refugees, driven there to make a valiant, last-ditch stand against marauding enemies?

Perhaps one day we shall know the answers to these and other tantalizing questions about the Negro builders of the silent cities of Africa.

8 The Sky-High Cities of Peru

Along the western coast of South America only a narrow strip of coastland separates the sea from the steep upward thrust of the mighty Andes. The mountains run in two parallel ranges, or cordilleras, for thousands of miles, with peaks soaring to nearly 25,000 feet. Between them lies a corridor of wild, barren land, tumbled by low traverse ranges of volcanic hills and gashed by narrow valleys.

There is the sierra, and its average height above sea level is 13,000 feet. Even the deepest of the valleys does not plunge below 7,000. It is a bleak and windswept land, too cold for any crop except potatoes or any animals except the native llamas and vicuñas. Frequently the earth is convulsed by volcanic eruptions and shuddering quakes. Yet this forbidding terrain was the cradle of two of the most powerful civilizations of Peru.

If we could follow the flight of the giant condor as it sweeps in lazy circles through the thin air, we might see that the sierra varies in width in its march from Ecuador to Argentina. At Cuzco, ancient capital of the Inca, it is no more than 200 miles across. Near the Bolivian border, however, it spreads out to 500, and the towering peaks serve as backdrops for the most fantastic lake in the world, Titicaca. The surface of this enormous body of water lies at 12,506 feet above sea level, making it the highest navigable lake on earth. It is so large that even the ocean-going steamers which ply its water seem to belong there.

Legend tells us that early in the thirteenth century of our era Mayta Capac, fourth Inca, led a mighty army of conquest southward to Lake Titicaca. Combining a little sightseeing with the business of war, the Inca took time out to visit the site of a ruined city near the lake shore. In doing so, he believed he was paying tribute to the memory of his ancestors, for Inca tradition held that Tiahuanaco was the birthplace of the Children of the Sun.

If Mayta Capac actually did visit the site, what he saw there must have been awe-inspiring indeed. The ruins of Tiahuanaco are impressive even today after seven centuries of further decay and destruction at the hands of nature and man.

The earliest written accounts we have come from the Spanish conquistadores, who visited the site soon after the conquest. Although their primary interest was in possible hoards of gold, a few were so struck by the wonders of the place that they left us their descriptions of it. Unfortunately, they were seldom in agreement about what they had seen, so that we find what is apparently the same building variously described as a fort, a temple, and a palace. Still others must have exaggerated on a rather grand scale, for modern archaeology has been unable to find any trace of some of the things they reported, though the scars of the Spanish search for gold are still in evidence.

If physical descriptions of the site fail to agree, how much more confusing will be the theories put forward to explain its existence? Such guesses have run the gamut from the mythical Atlantis and the ten lost tribes of Israel to a colony from outer space. Spanish priests pronounced the buildings and statues the work of the Prince of Darkness. Indian legends give the credit to the god of light, the sun god himself.

Actually, only one thing becomes clear from the chronicles. The Inca had nothing whatever to do with the building of Tiahuanaco. It was the creation of a distinctly different and much earlier people. But who were they? And when did they build their monuments?

The natives of the area offered a very simple explanation to the inquisitive Spaniards. The city, they said, had been built by a race of giants!

In Indian legends, the earth and its inhabitants were created by the god K'oni-tikki (Source of the Sun's Warmth). He became angered when men worshipped rocks, mountains, and rivers instead of their creator and punished them by sending a great flood to destroy all but a few. These he ordered to repopulate the earth, which they did.

But the new generations proved as blind and stubborn as the old. They paid homage to the high peaks, the caves, and other natural refuges which had saved mankind from destruction, angering the god anew. The furious K'oni-tikki turned them into the stone statues which can still be seen at Tiahuanaco.

Another version of the creation myth has it that the giants were only experimental, and that the god soon abandoned them in favor of men in his own image. It was arrogance and selfishness in man which brought the punishment of the deluge. Both legends end with an angry god striding off across the sea to the west.

It was these legends, combined with the strange similarity of Polynesian and Tiahuanacan monolithic statues, which led Thor Heyerdahl to make his famous voyage. The balsa raft on which he and his fellow scientists drifted across the lonely reaches of the Pacific was, of course, named *Kon-Tiki* in honor of the ancient god.

Under the name Viracocha (Swimmer on the Sea or Foam of the Sea), this god is the Peruvian counterpart of the Aztec Quetzalcoatl and the Mayan Kukulcan. All three were said to have been bearded *white* men who brought learning and civilization to the Indians, then sailed away in a ship with "swan wings" that looked like a gilded serpent gliding through the water. But before he left the white god always promised to return.

Needless to say, the bearded, white Spaniards profited immensely from this superstition, since they were often mistaken for the returning god. Long after the Peruvian conquest the Indians continued to address their Spanish masters as "Viracocha."

Though legends and farfetched theories abound, concrete facts about the ruins of Tiahuanaco have been a little harder to come by. The first qualified observer seems to have been Baron Alexander von Humboldt, who visited the site in 1802. It was he who first suggested that it might bear investigation for traces of a possible early culture. Few others had realized its importance except as a curiosity.

A German engineer, Arthur Posnansky, had tried to save some of the ruined buildings when they were being used as quarries for the construction of modern La Paz in Bolivia. Unfortunately, his plans and descriptions have not proved too reliable, and the poor man seems to have succeeded only in bringing the wrath of the archaeologists down on his own head. They accuse him of removing priceless evidence and falsifying his reports to make them fit in with his own pet theories.

By the time that truly scientific excavations began, many of the objects described by the early explorers had disappeared. The remainder had suffered much from repeated earthquakes and the carelessness of man. Only that which was too massive to be removed remains. Fortunately, that includes many of the most fascinating relics.

Foremost among them is a large pyramid with a flat top and an irregular trapezoidal base. It still stands roughly 65 feet high and must once have been much taller. Its builders used a 60-foot hill as a base for their structure. The three longer sides measure as much as 690 feet, making its basic dimensions only slightly smaller than those of the Great Pyramid in Egypt. And like that pyramid, this one seems to have been surrounded by smaller replicas.

The flat top contained a reservoir and the foundations of several buildings. The early chronicles stated that there were traces of steps leading from the summit to the edge of the lake which must have once been much higher. Today the ruins are miles from the nearest water.

Remains of
mysterious
Tiahuanaco —
found high in
the Andes —
unknown even
to the Incas.

Nearby is the Calasasaya, a tremendous court measuring 425 by 445 feet and surrounded by the remnants of the mighty, statue-adorned wall which once enclosed it. The main court is raised 13 feet from the ground, and in its center is an inner sunken court reached by a flight of steps composed of six colossal stone slabs. This may have been the holy of holies in the worship of the sun god himself.

Scattered thickly over the 125-acre site, huge statues stand or lie shattered and broken. Each was carved from a single block of stone. One, a red sandstone figure 24 feet tall, was discovered as late as 1932 by Dr. Wendell C. Bennett, who described it as "alien and forbidding."

There are two smaller enclosures, the Palacio and the Puma Puncu. Like the other monuments, these are constructed of tremendous stone blocks, some of them estimated to weigh more than 100 tons. The stones are carefully cut and dressed to fit together with scarcely a seam. A few well-built underground chambers have been discovered.

Possibly the most important among the monuments is the great stone gateway which stands majestic, alone, and leading nowhere. Known as the "Gateway of the Sun," this enormous sculpture is fashioned from a single slab of gray volcanic rock. It stands over 12½ feet wide and nearly 9 feet high. A square doorway has been cut through the 16-inch thickness at its center.

This monumental gateway faces east. When it was found, the massive lintel had been broken diagonally across, but in 1908 it was raised into place, and the break was repaired. Now the wonderful carvings which make this object so unique may be seen clearly once more.

The main figure is carved in high relief and stands facing forward in a haughty pose. He carries a staff as tall as he is in either hand. From his headdress sprout the heads of pumas and condors, symbols of mystic power, while from his belt dangles a fringe of human faces. This large central figure is surrounded by forty-eight smaller condor-headed figures marching in orderly array toward the god across the entire width of the gateway.

This monument with its carved figures is a supreme example of the type of art which at one time spread across the length and breadth of Peru from the high sierra to the coastal plains. It is known as the Tiahuanaco culture, and it set the style for decorations on everything from stone walls to pottery and textiles. Oddly enough, the only spot where it was not known was in the Cuzco area.

This widespread impact of the Tiahuanaco culture was once believed to have been due to military conquest. Today, however, more and more scholars tend to think that Tiahuanaco's influence was not political at all but religious. Only as the sacred city of a widespread and popular cult, whose worship was symbolized by the weeping sun god, could the barren, treeless land command the wealth and the labor of thousands which were necessary to build its great monuments.

Tiahuanaco stands at nearly 13,000 feet, an elevation that makes it virtually impossible for it to have produced food enough to support a large permanent population. Yet the labor of multitudes was required to move 100-ton blocks of stone from quarries three miles away without any means of transport other than man himself. Aside from these

common laborers, the building of the city also required
the services of large numbers of trained technicians, artists,
and artisans, who were undoubtedly fed by the work of
others. Only by drawing money, men, and supplies from
more fertile lands could the tremendous work have been
completed.

Why the forbidding *altiplano* was chosen as the site of
their Mecca by the Indians is not apparent, but it must
have been chosen at an early date. It is quite possible that
the area was occupied a few centuries before Christ. It did
not become important as a cult center, however, until the
fifth century A.D., and it only reached its zenith of power
during the period from A.D. 1000 to 1300.

It was then that the most impressive monuments were
erected. It was then that the holy city must have swarmed
with multitudes of the faithful whenever the major festivals
were held in honor of the sun god. It was a growing city,
throbbing and bustling with life.

And then, quite suddenly, the city was abandoned.

The evidence is everywhere. Temples under construction
were never completed. Statues, half carved, were never
finished. Great slabs of building stone were abandoned in
the quarries or along the roads. Why?

The reason for such hasty departure can only have been
fear. Were they fleeing before the military might of a conqueror? There is no evidence of that. Or were they inspired
with sudden terror and superstitious dread by a particularly
destructive earthquake? There is good evidence to support
this theory, and it seems for the moment to be the most
plausible explanation.

Whatever the reason, the city was abandoned, and its history was so completely forgotten that within a few short centuries no man could even guess who had built it. Only the vast piles of masonry and the terrifying statues remained.

Those, and the legends.

It is not at all surprising that a clever and enterprising people like the Inca should adopt those legends and use them to further their climb to power. According to Inca mythology, the first Inca ruler, Manco Capac, and his sister-wife were the first creations of Viracocha. Traditionally, they made their earthly appearance on the sacred Island of the Sun in the waters of Lake Titicaca, and every succeeding emperor was a pure and direct descendant of the Sun God. Certainly, to the ignorant and childlike minds of the Indians they were, indeed, the bright and shining Children of the Sun.

This divine and glorious descent was to prove of little use to the unfortunate Inca, Atahualpa, once Francisco Pizarro and his desperate and greedy Spaniards were allowed a glimpse of the fantastic treasures of his realm. Atahualpa, seized by the conquistadores, offered to ransom himself by filling a 25- by 15-foot room with gold. Pizarro agreed but later changed his mind and ordered the Inca murdered. Thereafter, the mighty empire fell like a ripe plum into the Spaniards' outstretched hands.

But in killing the Inca, they had overreached themselves. Once the word of his murder went out, the vast treasure that had been collected for his ransom disappeared forever into secret hiding places. Even so, there was enough gold and silver to make every half-starved conquistadore a millionaire ten times over.

In an effort to pacify the rebellious Indians, Pizarro set up Manco II, a relative of Atahualpa, as puppet ruler. Manco kept faith for a while, but in 1536 he rebelled against his Spanish overlords and founded the neo-Inca Empire. He fled to the Urubamba valley, where he was joined by an army of faithful subjects. After engaging the Spanish in several fierce battles, they retired to the Inca fortress of Ollantaytambo, but there was no safety even here.

Manco's troops were taken by surprise, and most of his family and all the sacred mummies of earlier emperors fell into enemy hands. Manco himself escaped to the mountains, where he managed to turn the tables on his pursuers. The Spaniards, already exhausted by marches at altitudes of over 15,000 feet, were caught in ambush and nearly annihilated.

Manco and his followers disappeared into the trackless mountains. The Emperor was soon afterward killed in a quarrel, but his sons carried on in his place. Not for many years would the last of them, Tupac Amaru, fall into the vengeful hands of the Spanish to be put to death "with fiendish cruelty."

The headquarters from which these neo-Inca Emperors ruled their scattered people was called Vilcabamba. Hidden away in the mountain fastnesses of the Andes, it was so well-guarded that no Spanish foe ever learned of its whereabouts and lived to tell the tale.

It was in search of this legendary capital that young Hiram Bingham of Yale prowled the rugged terrain around Cuzco in 1908 and again in 1911. Bingham had made the first arduous trip on muleback mainly to indulge a passion for mountain climbing, but the fascinating tales he heard soon had him wandering through 10,000-foot passes among 20,000-foot peaks in an effort to locate the last stronghold of the Incas.

He did find one ruined fortress hidden away in the mountains which he tentatively identified as Vitcos, an Inca city, but such a find only whetted his appetite for more. On the way back to Cuzco other ruins were pointed out to him, and three years later Bingham was back to explore them. During the course of this second journey his route led through the deep-cleft Urubamba valley.

There, while the rest of his party refreshed themselves by a swim in the river. Bingham and one Peruvian soldier followed a certain Melchior Arteaga across a slippery vine-and-log bridge. For Arteaga had promised to show him some unexplored ruins. Bingham had little hope of finding anything of importance so close to Cuzco, but he could not resist the invitation.

The way was incredibly steep and dangerous. Bingham found himself literally crawling his way up almost vertical cliffs made even more difficult by their festoons of jungle vegetation. By noon, they were nearly 2,000 feet above the river, and 8,000 feet above sea level. Here they met two Peruvian Indians who made their homes on those dizzying slopes and planted their little plots of maize and potatoes in tiny fields which were kept from sliding down the mountainside by stone retaining walls.

It took only a single glance at those well-built terraces

to convice Bingham they were of Inca origin. Eagerly he pushed on, careless now of the "tremendous green precipices" which everywhere yawned at his feet. Suddenly, he caught sight of buildings — buildings perched precariously on the brink of a gulf which plunged 2,000 feet straight down into the valley of the Urubamba!

Even from a distance Bingham could see that these were no crudely-built rock huts. They were as large and carefully constructed as those of Cuzco and much more graceful. One was semi-circular with a sloping outer wall. In Bingham's own words, this wall "followed the natural curvature of the rock and was keyed to it by one of the finest examples of masonry I had ever seen."

But he could not linger to marvel for long at one structure. There were others beyond, many of them. Bingham was now climbing upward along a vast granite staircase. At its top were two large buildings constructed of white-stone blocks, each higher than a man. The structures were roofless and boasted only three walls, the fourth side standing open.

Now Bingham noticed that the wall of one was set with three great windows looking east over the deep chasm. Something exciting clutched at his memory. He could almost see the words of the chronicle written in 1620 which told of an order given by Manco Capac. The Inca had commanded that certain works should be undertaken at the place of his birth, and that those works should include a masonry wall set with three windows!

Had he stumbled across the legendary Tampu Tocco, birthplace of the Children of the Sun?

Convinced that he had done just that, Bingham returned to Peru in 1912, backed by Yale University and the National Geographic Society, to excavate his lofty city. As it turned out, he found no evidence beyond the three windows to support his original theory, but he can hardly have been disappointed. What he did discover was fascinating enough.

For there, perched on the saddle running between two peaks known as Machu (old) and Huayna (new) Picchu, lay the ruins of a city whose existence had never before been suspected. No Inca legend or Spanish chronicle had ever so much as mentioned it. Yet, there it was with its temples and palaces, its peasant hovels and soldier's barracks, its plazas and terraces, just as it must have lain through all the years since the last Inca set foot there.

The site is breathtakingly beautiful. The city is set like a cameo among the vivid greens of the jungle-lush mountains. On every side rise the soaring peaks of the Andes, while the roaring Urubamba glitters like a silver thread at the bottom of the deep gorge.

Machu Picchu was a walled city, one of the very few known to Inca architecture. A single entrance pierced the wall which could be barred when necessary by a massive wooden gate — the supports and locking mechanism are still in evidence. Obviously it had been built with an eye to defense, and it could easily have withstood the most determined siege.

Many of the terraced fields lay within the walls, ensuring a supply of food, and water was brought in stone aqueducts from the heights a mile away. Running through the heart of the city was the so-called stairway of the fountains.

Water from the aqueduct was led into a series of sixteen descending basins to spout clear and cold from level to level and furnish the needs of the populace. There was also a complex irrigation system for the terraced crops.

Such precautions seem almost unnecessary when the nearly impregnable defenses of nature are considered. It is certain that not even their most formidable enemy, the Spanish, could ever have carried the place by storm, assuming they could have found it to begin with.

Which brings us to the greatest mystery of all. Why build a walled city in such an inaccessible place? Why expend the incredible labor required to drag enormous stones up a steep mountainside? What purpose could such a city serve?

There are many theories. The American explorer, Victor von Hagen, believes that Machu Picchu was no more than the final link in a long chain of what he calls "hanging cities" which stretched along the Urubamba. Their purpose? To protect the Inca Empire from the raids of the wild jungle tribes to the east of the mountain range.

Others believe that here, so close to Cuzco yet so well hidden, was the final refuge of the sacred virgins of the Inca religion, the Brides of the Sun. The fact that the skeletal remains which have been recovered there are mostly of females lends some color to this theory. Surely the site had some religious significance.

It is approached along the terraced mountainside by a flight of stone steps. (In all there are more than one hundred stairways at Machu Picchu with over three thousand steps.) The buildings rise tier on tier, culminating at the highest point with a strange and much debated flat stone and obelisk. This is assumed to have had some astronomical, hence religious, purpose, possibly serving as a crude sundial. It is called *Intihuatana,* the Tethering Place of the Sun.

Finally, there is the belief held by Bingham himself that here at last was the stronghold of the neo-Inca state, Vilcabamba. If this is the true explanation, Machu Picchu saw the final end of one of the greatest of pre-Colombian civilizations. Here was the place where the Inca power still held sway nearly one hundred years after the empire had fallen. Here was the tiny backwater where the ancient customs were still followed, and the ancient gods were still honored.

Hidden away from the prying eyes of the world and completely self-sufficient, it might have held out for centuries more. Instead, it was abandoned. Why?

Perhaps, with the last Inca gone, executed by the Spanish in 1572, there was nothing left to fight for. Perhaps, as Bingham believed, the water supply was disrupted by an earthquake, leaving the city to die of thirst.

Whatever the reason, no sound and fury of battle marks the final end of the mighty empire of the Inca. No mournful funeral dirge denotes its passing. No sound awakens the echoes of history— nothing but the whisper of a sandaled foot along the stone stairways and the faint creaking of the heavy gate as it swings open for the very last time.

And the jungle vines creep silently along the crumbling walls of still another silent city.

Bibliography

Bingham, Hiram, *Lost City of the Incas*. New York, Duell, Sloan and Pearce, 1948.

Bloch, Raymond, *The Etruscans*. New York, Frederick A. Praeger, 1958

Breasted, James Henry, *A History of Egypt*. New York, Bantam Books, 1964 (first published by Scribner's, 1905)

Cleator, P. E., *Lost Languages*. London, Robert Hale, Limited, 1959

Cles-Reden, Sibylle von, *The Buried People*. New York, Charles Scribner's Sons, 1956

Cottrell, Leonard, *The Anvil of Civilization*. New York, Mentor Books, 1957; *Lost Cities,* Holt, Rinehart and Winston, Inc., New York, 1957; *The Golden Book of Lost Worlds*. New York, Golden Press, 1963

Cottrell, Leonard, *The Bull of Minos*. New York, Holt, Rinehart and Winston, 1953

Cottrell, Leonard, *The Lost Pharaohs*. New York, Grosset & Dunlap, 1961

Creel, Herrlee Glessner, *The Birth of China*. New York, Frederick Ungar Publishing Co., 1937

Crump, Irving and James, *Dragon Bones in the Yellow Earth.*

Dales, George F., "The Decline of the Harappans." *Scientific American 1935* CCXIV, Number 5, (May, 1966), 92-100

De la Vega, Garcilaso, *The Incas*. New York, The Orion Press, 1961

Davidson, Basil, *Lost Cities of Africa*. Boston, Little, Brown and Company, 1959

Fairservis, Walter A., *The Ancient Kingdoms of the Nile*. New York, Thomas Y. Crowell, 1962

Fairservis, Walter, *Origins of Oriental Civilization*. Mentor

Gurney, O. R., *The Hittites*. Baltimore, Penguin Books, 1952

Hagen, Victor W. von, *Realm of the Incas*. New York, Mentor Books, 1957

Heurgon, Jacques, *Daily Life of the Etruscans*. New York, The Macmillan Company, 1964

Honoré, Pierre, *In Quest of the White God*. New York, G. P. Putnam's Sons, 1964

Leicht, Herman, *Pre-Inca Art and Culture*.

Lloyd, Seton, *Early Anatolia*. Baltimore, Penguin Books, 1956

Mackay, Ernest, *The Indus Civilization*. London, Lovat Dickson & Thompson Ltd.

Mason, J. Alden, *The Ancient Civilizations of Peru*. Baltimore, Penguin Books, 1957

The National Geographic Society, *Everyday Life in Ancient Times*. Washington, D. C., The National Geographic Society, 1951

Piggott, Stuart, *Prehistoric India*. New York, Barnes & Noble, Inc. 1962

Prescott, William, *The Conquest of Peru*.

Richardson, Emeline, *The Etruscans*. Chicago, University of Chicago Press, 1964

Samachson, Dorothy and Joseph, *Good Digging*. New York, Rand McNally, 1960.

Schreiber. Hermann and Georg, *Vanished Cities*. New York, Alfred A. Knopf, 1957

Silverberg, Robert, *Empires in the Dust*, Philadelphia, Chilton Books, 1963; *Lost Cities and Vanished Civilizations*, Philadelphia, Chilton Books, 1962

Smith, William Stevenson, *Ancient Egypt*. Boston, Museum of Fine Arts, 1960

Summers, Roger, *Zimbabwe: A Rhodesian Mystery*. Johannesburg, Thomas Nelson and Sons, 1963

White, Anne Terry, *Lost Worlds*. New York, Random House, 1941
Woolley, Sir Leonard, *The Beginnings of Civilization*. New York, Mentor Books, 1965

Index